McKinsey Quarterly

2010 Number 3

This Quarter

Trends matter, even slow and steady ones like demography or productivity, and missing them can be costly: think streaming media and music producers. Systematically spotting and acting on emerging trends, on the other hand, helps firms capture market opportunities, test risks, develop capabilities, and spur innovation. Companies in industries ranging from insurance to retailing to energy production are doing just that in embracing the growing concern about climate change. What's more, a host of new companies are in effect being "born global"—exploiting a web of trade, sourcing, and connectivity that didn't exist 20 years ago.

For much of the past year, a team at McKinsey has revisited our assumptions about the global trends that will define the coming era. We have identified five crucibles where the stresses and tensions will be greatest and thus offer the richest opportunities for companies to innovate and adapt. This issue provides an overview of all five and treats in depth one of them: the "great rebalancing" of economic activity to developing markets. It also contains a glimpse of new thinking about how to disaggregate broad trends into highly granular, industry-specific implications.

We start with China, where, despite the tremendous growth prospects, many companies still treat the market as an interesting side bet. "Building a second home in China" proposes an alternative approach that involves bolder aspirations, better execution, and intense localization. China also is the setting for "Applying global trends: A look at China's auto industry," which uses an intriguing example—the speed with which Chinese automakers could penetrate developed markets—to lay out a methodology for assessing global trends in a scenario-based planning process. Strategists who apply such approaches boost their odds of spotting the next big opportunity or threat before it's apparent to everyone else.

China is far from the only important emerging market. India is urbanizing at a breakneck pace, as "India's urban transformation," the "Picture This" graphic spread, depicts. In total, nearly two billion consumers across 12 emerging economies currently spend roughly $7 trillion a year, and this figure is growing fast. To keep up with that growth while achieving meaningful scale, "Capturing the world's emerging middle class" explains that companies must identify clusters of consumers across multiple markets. And this isn't a game just for Western multinationals: new competitors are exploding from emerging markets, often finding ready customers in developed markets as well.

The great rebalancing may not be smooth and orderly. "Globalization's critical imbalances" enumerates the growing tensions in global currency, commodity, and debt markets arising from the fact that capital is mobile but labor is largely fixed. An abrupt realignment of world currencies could dramatically affect the attractiveness of many global operations.

Even the most talented strategists will have, at best, incomplete knowledge of what comes next. What's certain is that developing an informed view of the forces that will define the future provides the best chance for shaping it.

Peter Bisson is a director in McKinsey's Stamford office.

On the cover

How to compete in a rebalancing global economy

Features

Departments

On Our Web Site

What's driving Africa's growth

This examination of Africa's growth prospects headlines an extensive series of articles, interviews, and multimedia that explores Africa's new profile on the world stage.

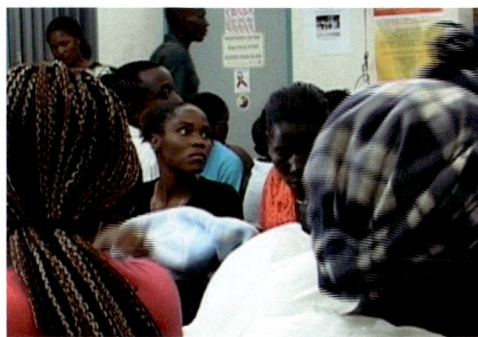

Improving maternal health in Namibia: An inside look

Tour a pilot project in Namibia's capital, where simple, scalable actions are saving mothers' lives.

Video

Other features:

McKinsey conversations with global leaders: David Rubenstein of The Carlyle Group

A founding managing director of The Carlyle Group reflects on the future of the private-equity industry.

Video

How to test your decision-making instincts

Executives should trust their gut instincts—but only when four tests are met.

Video and audio podcasts on iTunes

Download conversations with executives and authors in audio or video from iTunes.

mckinseyquarterly.com/itunes

Join the *McKinsey Quarterly* community on Facebook

facebook.com/mckinseyquarterly

Follow us on Twitter

Receive notification of new articles by following @McKQuarterly on Twitter.

Idea Exchange

Readers mix it up with authors of articles from *McKinsey Quarterly*
2010, Number 2

Seeing through biases in strategic decisions

The cover package in the last issue of *McKinsey Quarterly* focused on how cognitive biases can undermine strategic decision making and included suggestions from a variety of thought leaders on how to minimize the damage that biases inflict.

Presented here are five elements of the conversation that occurred on mckinseyquarterly.com regarding this topic. It includes comments from readers and responses from Nobel Laureate Daniel Kahneman, cognitive psychologist Gary Klein, Kleiner Perkins partner Randy Komisar, and McKinsey's Olivier Sibony.

Is strategy formulation arbitrary?

If good methods were available, biases, power relations, and other social issues would drop away, since it would be obvious that an idea did or did not make sense. We don't see process dominating how engineers build bridges or how accountants prepare financial statements, so why is it acceptable that the biggest corporate decisions of all—on strategy—depend on such arbitrary processes?

Kim Warren
Director, Strategy Dynamics, London

McKinsey's Olivier Sibony responds:
Kim, we do in fact see process dominate how engineers build bridges and how accountants prepare statements. These processes include and embody methods and tools that are known to deliver "acceptable" solutions. If I understand your point, it's that there is no real method for strategy formulation. At present, you're right—there is no universally accepted method known to deliver a superior strategy in all situations; or rather, there are so many that figuring out which one to use in what situation requires a lot of skill and judgment, which boils down to the same thing.

So the question remains: what to do? Our argument is that in the absence of a generally accepted and foolproof method to make strategic decisions, a process that confronts as many ideas and judgments as possible will at least help.

Do cognitive biases cross cultures?

This is a good article, but there is one glaring omission: coping with the enormous differences in decision making that you find in differing national cultures. Even though one of the tips wisely recommends to "make the team as diverse as possible," this, and the other tips, assume a common national culture. This is often not the case, especially in multinationals with multiple global locations.

Leo Salazar
Senior program director, De Baak Management Center, Amsterdam

Olivier Sibony responds:

Mr. Salazar, this seems to be a common concern, as I've heard it many times over from both clients and journalists. As demonstrated by years of experiments in all cultures, cognitive biases are universal; therefore the general principles that combat them are also universal. What does, and should, vary according to national culture—and by corporate culture, as we point out in the article—are the tools and techniques you use to put these principles into practice. It is fair to assume, for instance, that the ways in which an American executive encourages dissent (or tries to) might not be effective in some Asian countries.

Can simple tests help executives decide when to trust intuition?

Andrew Campbell and Jo Whitehead, directors at the Ashridge Business School in London, wrote a short essay, published in full on mckinseyquarterly.com, in response to the conversation Daniel Kahneman and Gary Klein had regarding when executives should and should not trust intuition. A short excerpt from the essay follows.

Because the latest findings in decision neuroscience suggest that we simply can't get away from the influence of our gut instincts, we've developed the following four tests to help tell when we can trust our gut feelings.

1. Familiarity test: Are we dealing with a familiar issue? Our instincts will be a good guide if our experience is appropriate. We need to look at the uncertainties in the situation and assess whether we have sufficient experience to make good judgments about each uncertainty.

2. Feedback test: Without clear feedback, we may not have learned the right lessons from past decisions. If in past situations we moved jobs before the impact of the decision was clear or people protected us from bad news, our gut may be sending us the wrong messages.

3. Measured-emotions test: Our instincts can be unbalanced by particularly strong emotions. If we have had especially good or especially bad outcomes in similar situations, we cannot rely on our gut instincts.

4. Independence test: Do we have personal interests or attachments at stake in this situation? If so, our subconscious will be unable to remain objective. Our instincts will be biased by the emotions triggered by these interests. For example, if we are trying to decide between two office locations for our organization—one of which is much more personally convenient—our gut feelings may well mislead us.

Daniel Kahneman, Nobel laureate and professor emeritus of psychology and public affairs at Princeton University's Woodrow Wilson School, responds:

I enjoyed the essay by Campbell and Whitehead, which is highly compatible with the position that Gary and I reached and adds two danger signs—emotional involvement and personal interest—that we did not consider. The one important difference between our approaches is that Campbell and Whitehead address their advice to executives who may wish to question their own intuitions. We dealt with a much easier question: when should one trust *someone else's* intuitions?

The difference is significant. I see little reason to believe that individuals can follow advice to second-guess themselves—even if the advice is compelling and well documented. It is much easier to second-guess someone else. My skepticism about the efficacy of advice is also the reason for my enthusiasm about Gary's idea of the premortem. The premortem is a low-cost procedure that does not require self-doubt or self-control from anyone and could plausibly be adopted by an organization and become a routine. To conclude, I would certainly include the four tests listed by Campbell and Whitehead as part of what I call an effort at quality control over decisions, but I believe this effort must involve other people as well as the actual decision maker.

Will efforts to avert disaster stifle innovation?

Gary Klein's suggestion that managers conduct "premortems"—in which, before starting a project, team members imagine it was a fiasco and write down all the reasons why—caught the attention of several readers. One commented:

The idea of a premortem sounds interesting, but in a creative environment I would worry that it is more likely to lead to turning down ideas or to paralysis: it seems to be a process of finding reasons why not rather than reasons why. It is always much easier to find problems than to find positives.

Giles Keeble
London, UK

Gary Klein, a cognitive psychologist and senior scientist at MacroCognition, responds:
There is a trade-off between encouraging new ideas and providing critical evaluation of them. We need to do both. I don't imagine that Mr. Keeble is suggesting that ideas be turned into plans that should be implemented without any evaluation. The premortem is simply a way to accomplish the evaluation efficiently and effectively. It is also a way to reduce overconfidence.

Mr. Keeble is correctly raising the concern that a premortem might be too effective and diminish confidence to a point that the morale of the team suffers. We also worry about that effect. The last activity in premortem sessions is to ask the team members to look at the concerns they have identified and then to have each team member volunteer one action that he or she will take to reduce the chance that the plan will lead to a fiasco. My experience is that this final premortem activity establishes team commitment—a commitment that is now based on a more thoughtful assessment of the plan, and a commitment that is more credible given the demonstration of the team members that they are willing to speak up about the things that worry them.

A 'balance sheet' for complex decisions?

Randy Komisar makes some fabulous points. I love his "balance sheet" idea, to assemble a diverse group and then have them list points on both sides of a difficult decision, without explicitly stating their positions. However, I realize now that this idea only works if you are in a go/no-go situation. If you have a complex problem with multiple options, you can only engage the balance sheet tool once you have arrived at a view about which is the best option. By this stage, you may have anchored on your earlier judgments making it harder to use the tools.

Andrew Campbell
Director, Ashridge Business School, London
(McKinsey alumnus)

Kleiner Perkins partner Randy Komisar responds:

Thank you, Andrew, your comment is a good one. You are right that, clearly, it is easier to apply the balance sheet approach in go/no-go decisions. But it can also be applied to more complex decisions as well, many of which can be effectively parsed into forking go/no-go decisions.

The balance sheet actually serves as a reflection of complexity, even when the decision is first posed as a binary one. For example, a complex decision about how to structure a transaction might be posed as a go/no-go on the extreme scenarios—debt or equity. But the balance sheet illuminates the nuances of the more complex structuring and hones the debate on the options (more debt, less equity; long-term debt versus short-term debt; and so on).

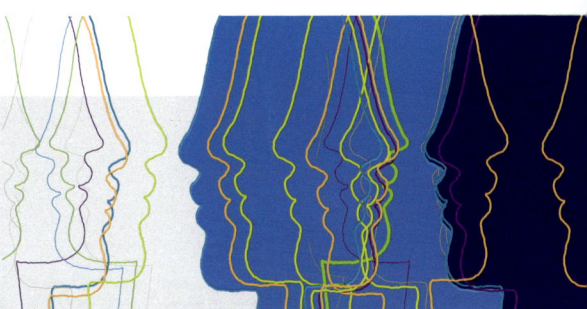

Measuring word-of-mouth marketing

Another article in our last issue focused on the opportunities and measurement challenges associated with word-of-mouth marketing. One reader commented:

The article speaks about "word-of-mouth equity"—the index of a brand's power to create messages that influence a consumer to make purchases. But focusing on this solves only half the issue. What about an index that measures the consumer's capability of being influential? Wouldn't it be even more important to know whom to target?

Michael Klausner
CMO, Groupable, New York

McKinsey's Jonathan Doogan responds:

Great question, Michael. I agree that an index that measures a consumer's influence would be very valuable. In a sense, P&G's Tremor—a word-of-mouth marketing organization that has, among other things, recruited influential teenagers to test new marketing approaches and products to get real-time feedback and to generate buzz—has this underlying formula. Such a formula would likely contain demographic, attitudinal, and behavioral characteristics, which receivers find compelling. This mix of characteristics will vary significantly by category (and receiver segment), but some underlying principles, we propose, are the propensity to talk credibly or knowledgably in the category, status as a purchaser or early adopter, and whether or not the potential influencers have a network of "listeners." How a marketer finds these people is another question—and is more or less challenging depending on the data richness and the influencers' willingness to engage.

 Visit our Web site at **mckinseyquarterly.com** to read comments from our readers on these and other articles—or share your own.

Capturing the world's emerging middle class

David Court and Laxman Narasimhan

Multinational companies need new "scale at speed" approaches to penetrate the developing world's increasingly prosperous consumer markets.

David Court is a director in McKinsey's Dallas office, and Laxman Narasimhan is a director in the Delhi office.

The rapidly growing ranks of middle-class consumers span a dozen emerging nations, not just the fast-growing BRIC countries,[1] and include almost two billion people, spending a total of $6.9 trillion annually. Our research suggests that this figure will rise to $20 trillion during the next decade—about twice the current consumption in the United States.

These new spenders offer an opportunity for early winners to gain lasting advantages, just as companies in Europe and the United States did at similar points in their development. In 17 product categories in the United States, for example, we found that the market leader in 1925 remained the number-one or number-two player for the rest of the century. These companies include Kraft Foods (Nabisco), which led in biscuits; Del Monte Foods, in canned fruit; and Wrigley, in chewing gum.

Despite having strong global brands, multinational companies face challenging competition in emerging markets, as these economies already boast aggressive local players that have captured a significant por-tion of spending. Chinese beverage maker Hangzhou Wahaha, for example, has built a $5.2 billion business against global competitors such as Coca-Cola and PepsiCo by targeting rural areas, filling product gaps that meet local needs, keeping costs low, and appealing to patriotism.

Further complicating matters is the fact that the multinationals' business models are based on practices established in the markets of the developed world, where the game is won slowly by finding cost savings and making product improvements that capture single percentage points of market share over time. Among emerging markets, perhaps only China can provide enough short-term growth to justify that strategy. Meeting the needs of most consumers in emerging markets requires a different course, which often elicits anguished cries in the corridors of the multinationals: "You want me to change my business model and go across the world for $50 million in revenue?" It's an understandable lament for executives who not only fear ending up with little to show for their efforts but also are wary of the battles already under way among emerging-market champions.

While there are multiple approaches to capturing emerging-market consumers, the two critical factors are speed and scale. Our experience suggests that one way multinationals can quickly gain the scale they need is to identify clusters of similar consumers across multiple markets. That approach allows these companies to build revenue and profit streams that are collectively material and justify significant, ongoing capital investments to fuel growth. Another tack is to work at a more local level, gaining scale in specific regions and

In developing countries, the emerging class—nearly two billion strong—spends a total of $6.9 trillion annually.

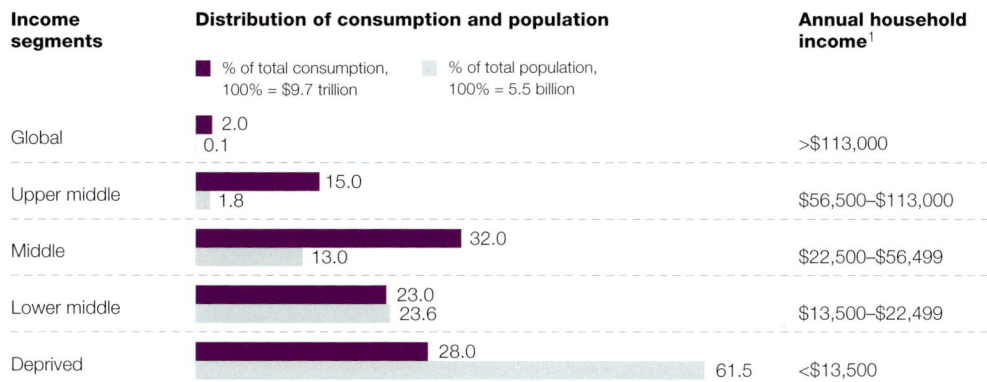

Income segments	Distribution of consumption and population	Annual household income[1]
	■ % of total consumption, 100% = $9.7 trillion ▪ % of total population, 100% = 5.5 billion	
Global	2.0 / 0.1	>$113,000
Upper middle	15.0 / 1.8	$56,500–$113,000
Middle	32.0 / 13.0	$22,500–$56,499
Lower middle	23.0 / 23.6	$13,500–$22,499
Deprived	28.0 / 61.5	<$13,500

[1]Based on purchasing-power-adjusted exchange rate.

Note: Developing countries are Argentina, Brazil, Chile, China, Colombia, Egypt, India, Indonesia, Iran, Malaysia, Mexico, Nigeria, Pakistan, Peru, the Philippines, Poland, Romania, Russia, South Africa, Thailand, Turkey, Ukraine, Venezuela, Vietnam.

Source: Economist Intelligence Unit, June 2009; Euromonitor, June 2009; World Bank, April 2009; McKinsey analysis

categories by teaming up with deeply knowledgeable on-the-ground partners. They can help not only in product development but also in distribution and market positioning—the crucial final steps to reaching highly local consumer markets.

All of this is easier said than done, of course, because consumers in emerging markets are extremely diverse. In some ways, they resemble those in developed nations: they are aware of and have a fondness for brands and want access to a variety of products at different prices, including products they aspire to but can't currently afford. Yet their tastes are often localized, and while they are middle-class in regional terms,[2] they are still not wealthy enough to replace products regularly, because their percentage of truly discretionary income is lower: in China and India, for example, about 40 percent of average household income is spent on food and transportation, compared with 25 percent in the United States.

The best way to make sense of this picture is to take a granular view using product categories. For individual categories, multinationals should first identify whether consumer needs in emerging markets are fundamentally global or local. A good proxy for this issue is the similarity of product offerings across geographies, as shown on the horizontal axis of the exhibit below. Second, multinationals can assess the consumer's ability to afford a given product. Useful approximations include category penetration and product availability in key developing markets, as well as the willingness of consumers to "stretch"

Four category-specific strategies can help companies serve middle-class consumers in developing markets.

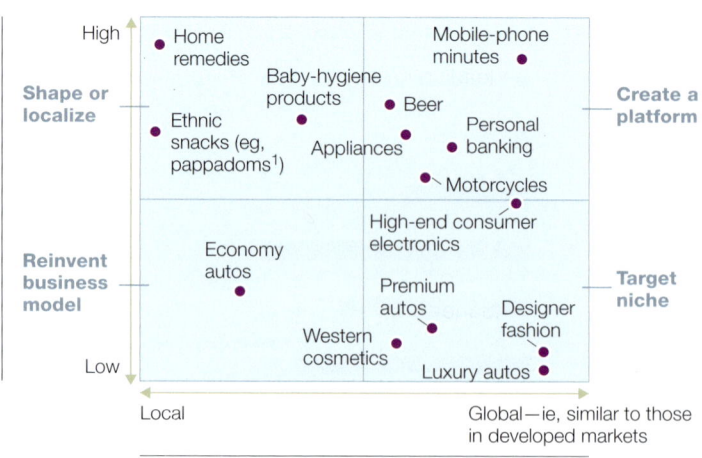

Middle-class consumers' ability to buy
- Affordability (disposable income, product costs, and willingness to 'stretch')
- Accessibility (product distribution)

Middle-class consumers' needs
(expressed, not latent)

[1] Spicy, wafer-thin Indian bread.

to buy less-affordable products. By developing a perspective on whether and to what extent consumer tastes are global or local and combining that with a clear view on the affordability and accessibility of a given product, multinationals can go a long way toward determining the strategies and business models that will allow them to gain scale quickly.

Identifying consumers with similar needs across markets

The first category, at the top right of the matrix, comprises products and services for which consumer needs are quite similar across geographies and affordability is not a constraint. There is little need to create marketing plans to roll out such products in different countries, one after another: we've found that it's most efficient to identify similar consumer segments across countries and to build scalable business models for each cluster. Examples of products in this category include personal banking, mobile communications, consumer electronics, and pharmaceuticals, which have similar industry structures, rates of consumer adoption, and socioreligious factors across geographies.

A leading multinational retail bank's marketing team, for example, used longitudinal consumer data to identify five clusters across multiple Asian countries. These segments included one of conservative users very loyal to their local banks (in India, Indonesia, the Philippines, and Taiwan) and another of remote-channel users who were highly price sensitive (in Hong Kong, Singapore, and South Korea). The bank successfully designed and implemented a specific product and channel strategy for each of these five segments across countries.

Targeting premium consumers in product niches

The category on the bottom right of the matrix comprises emerging-market consumers who have the means to buy products and services that are widely available or even mass market in the developed world. (For the vast majority of the emerging middle class, however, these products and services are neither affordable nor accessible—they are premium items.) While we forecast that less than 3 percent of total emerging-market households will be in this bottom-right category in 2025, their prosperity and the fact that their behavior resembles that of consumers in the developed world has historically made this category appealing to multinationals.

Capturing the loyalty of these consumers and, as they develop new needs, upgrading them is the key. Since emerging-market consumers want value—even in this category—companies should offer products at "mass premium" price points. Consumer electronics manufacturer LG has found that people in many developing markets are more willing to pay for better service than are their counterparts in the developed world. The company launched a premium offering that not only gives consumers a full-time contact person who acts as a go-between with LG and monitors the health of products but also guarantees maintenance visits within 6 hours (compared with the normal 24-hour commitment).

Shaping the market by localizing

The third category, on the top left of the matrix, comprises affordable and accessible products, such as low-cost snacks and highly localized baby-care hygiene products.

In this category, there's clear merit in evaluating how companies can scale up across markets, even if needs are local. One approach is to shape the market through minor product enhancements and sharper positioning that encourages consumers to shift toward more globally convergent offerings over time and allows companies to enjoy greater economies of scale and lower delivery costs. In India, for example, PepsiCo successfully shaped the snack market by creating a new platform, called Kurkure, for younger consumers. The product feels entirely local, though it is packaged and distributed by Frito-Lay.

Other strategies for penetrating this affordable, accessible, and local market are to use celebrity endorsements and to leverage local knowledge, either selectively, in areas such as distribution, or through more comprehensive alliances. The partnership between Norwegian telecommunications company Telenor and Bangladesh's Grameen Telecom, for example, resulted in the creation, in 1997, of Grameen Phone, now the country's largest mobile operator.

Reinventing the business model

The final category, on the bottom left of the matrix, represents products and services for which needs are (and will probably remain) very local and affordability is a challenge. In this segment, the potential available market share is high, though the market looks small, since consumers often substitute cheaper products, from adjacent categories, that satisfy similar needs rather than buy a higher-priced global product. The first step for multinationals is to define the market by measuring current total consumption, examining product alternatives that satisfy similar needs, and studying potential spending likely to be unlocked once incomes grow. Companies then need to make their products more affordable and accessible, looking at everything from capital expenditures to product features to distribution. There's real value in working with local players to drive product, distribution, and sales innovations in that "last mile" before reaching consumers.

Beer manufacturer SABMiller, for example, decided it could not achieve price points that would spur demand in Africa without changing its business model. It retooled its factories for cheaper, locally sourced ingredients (such as cassava and sugar rather than barley and maize) and used local distributors to ensure the availability of its products. The result: lower prices, growing demand, and significant increases in market share across several African countries.

Traditional approaches in which companies enter markets one by one and focus on a handful of brand and market combinations will not meet the challenges of the developing world's large and growing body of middle-class consumers. Companies need to become adept at building and sharing customer information across markets and more willing to work with others to gain scale quickly. In some regions, such as Africa, multinationals may even need to work with the public and social sector to ensure that consumers have adequate income to generate demand.

Structural changes might also be required. Because multinationals may have to adopt different business models by market, category, and brand, they need flexible and responsive organizations. Cisco, for example, has created a second world headquarters, in India, to spearhead its push into the country, while other companies are establishing centers of excellence to identify, recruit, and develop staff that can be deployed locally. Using local vendors is critical to running a lean operation: many multinationals have found, for example, that capital outlays in emerging markets are often only 30 percent of those required for a factory in the West if they use local resources for plant and process engineering and to execute projects.

Finally, companies need to be aware of perhaps the biggest bottleneck to seizing the emerging middle-class opportunity: talent. Relying excessively on expatriates is likely to stifle an organization's ability to scale up adequately across markets—there simply won't be enough staff. We believe that building talent academies inside companies to accelerate leadership development is a good step. Yet the rapid growth in many emerging markets may make traditional "grow your own" or "hire from within" approaches manifestly inadequate to meet staffing needs. By addressing these structural and operational imperatives and identifying the best approaches to achieve the scale needed to serve the growing middle class, multinationals can meet their high expectations for international growth. o

The authors would like to acknowledge the contributions of Georges Desvaux, Vinay Dixit, Martin Elling, John Forsyth, Prashant Gandhi, Trond Riiber Knudsen, Vikram Vaidyanathan, and Ireena Vittal to this article.

[1] Brazil, Russia, India, and China.
[2] We define *emerging middle-class consumers* as those with yearly incomes of $13,500 to $113,000, in purchasing-power-parity terms.

Older, smarter, more value conscious: The French consumer transformation

Georges Desvaux and Baudouin Regout

Long-term trends reshaping the consumer landscape in France have implications for other developed countries too.

Georges Desvaux is a director in McKinsey's Paris office; Baudouin Regout, who is based in Brussels, is a senior fellow of the McKinsey Global Institute.

Over the next 20 years, powerful demographic, societal, and economic trends promise to reshape consumer behavior substantially in many of the world's wealthier nations. The implications for business will be significant. To better understand how these trends will play out, McKinsey's Consumer and Shopper Insights Center, with the support of the McKinsey Global Institute, examined the prospects of France and found that there, as in many of its European neighbors, the average household in 2030 will be older, better educated, and less wealthy than the average household today.

We found three long-term trends reaching a tipping point that will fun-

The average French household in 2030 will look very different than it does today.

	Demographic change		**Societal change** (ages 15 to 54 years)	
	# of households	Average age of individuals	Individuals who attained tertiary degree (out of 10 individuals)	Individuals who are coupled (out of 10 households)
1980	19 million	36 years	1	7
2007	27 million	40 years	2	6
2030	33 million	43 years	4	6

damentally transform the country: an aging population, societal shifts altering what households look like, and economic factors slowing the expansion of wealth. As these trends sweep across France and, to varying degrees, the rest of Europe, they will impose pressure on consumption growth and dramatically change the consumer landscape.

A transforming nation

France's population is getting older as longevity rises, fertility rates fall, and the large baby boom generation ages. These trends have profound economic implications, pressuring per capita GDP growth, purchasing power, and consumption. We expect that by 2030, for example, more than half of all French households will be headed by someone aged 55 or older. Across Europe, just two workers will support each retiree by 2050,

compared with four today, unless the retirement age changes.

A range of societal shifts are reshaping the average French household. These include rising educational attainment, more women participating in the labor market, and smaller households as fewer couples form them and the birthrate declines. We forecast that the number of French households with couples who live together will fall to 58 percent in 2030, from 75 percent in 1980, while households will have an average of 2.5 children, down from 3.3 in 1980.

The final transformational factor is economic. Since World War II, an expanding European economy has allowed successive generations to earn more and accumulate greater net worth than previous gen-

Economic change
(real 2000 euros)

Households have on average . . .	Households' average earning and spending	Out-of-pocket medical	Electronics	Gasoline
 **3.3 members** **1.1 children**	 **€33,300 earned** **€27,300 spent**	 **€440**	**€130**	**€1,300**
 **2.6 members** **0.8 children**	 **€41,200 earned** **€34,700 spent**	**€1,290**	**€1,700**	**€1,060**
 **2.5 members** **0.8 children**	 **€48,300 earned** **€40,900 spent**	**€2,140**	**€4,080**	**€1,040**

erations had. This trend will continue, but at a slower pace as economic and consumption growth slow dramatically because of the aging population (which will cut overall workforce participation), weaker productivity gains, and the rising cost of limited resources, notably oil. In the absence of government reforms and major policy changes, we expect annual GDP growth in France to be 1.5 percent from 2008 to 2030, down from 2.1 percent from 1980 to 2008.

What it means

As a result of these factors, we believe that the annual growth of consumption in France (after housing and utilities) will fall to 1.4 percent in the next two decades, compared with 2 percent between 1980 and 2007. As an aggregate market, the mature-consumer segment—those aged 55 or older—will dominate by virtue of sheer numbers, accounting for around two-thirds of all additional consumption in the period to 2030. People aged 65 or older will account for almost half of that. These older households, however, will individually be less wealthy than the rest of the population and will continue to seek value.

Mature French consumers will account for a majority of total spending increases over the coming decades.

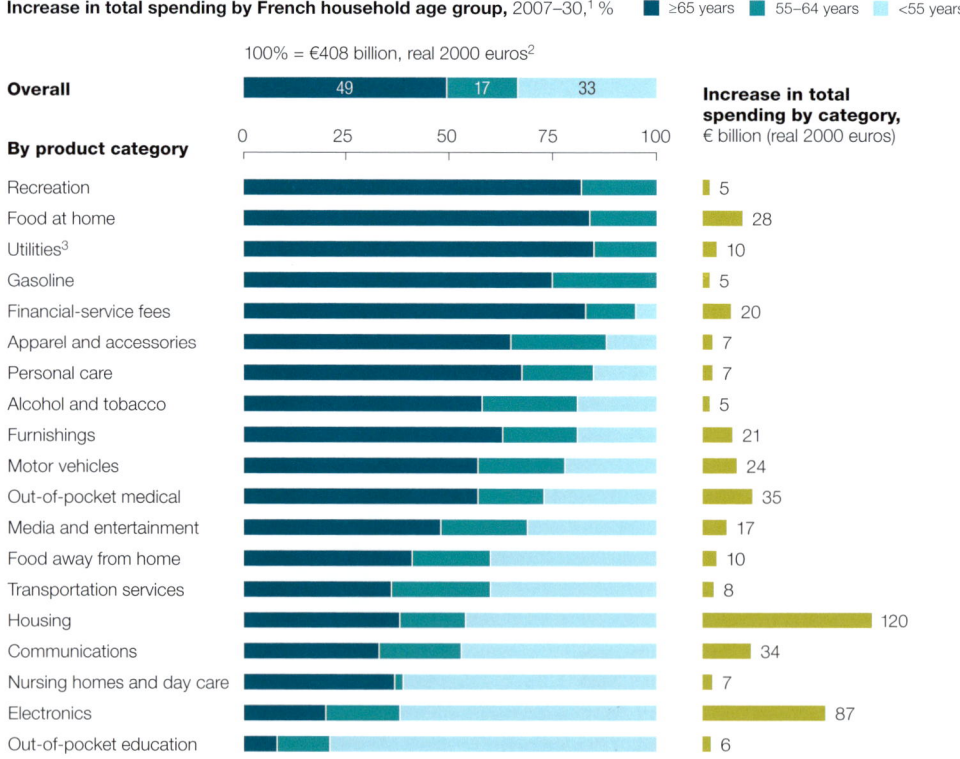

Increase in total spending by French household age group, 2007–30,[1] %   ≥65 years   55–64 years   <55 years

100% = €408 billion, real 2000 euros[2]

Overall	49	17	33

Increase in total spending by category, € billion (real 2000 euros)

By product category		Increase in total spending (€ billion)
Recreation		5
Food at home		28
Utilities[3]		10
Gasoline		5
Financial-service fees		20
Apparel and accessories		7
Personal care		7
Alcohol and tobacco		5
Furnishings		21
Motor vehicles		24
Out-of-pocket medical		35
Media and entertainment		17
Food away from home		10
Transportation services		8
Housing		120
Communications		34
Nursing homes and day care		7
Electronics		87
Out-of-pocket education		6

[1] Projected; mature households aged 55 and over account for >100% of additional spending in recreation, food at home, utilities, and gasoline, since they compensate for lower consumption by younger age groups.
[2] Figures do not sum to 100%, because of rounding.
[3] Electricity, heating materials (eg, coal, wood), natural gas, and water.

We expect annual GDP growth in France to be 1.5 percent from 2008 to 2030, down from 2.1 percent from 1980 to 2008.

For business, the dynamics of product growth will vary widely from category to category—and there will be winners and losers. Categories with above-average growth per household will be electronics, out-of-pocket medical expenses, communications, and housing. Those with stable growth include media and entertainment, energy, and personal care. Spending on the maintenance and repair of dwellings will decline. Combined with changing consumer aspirations, this growth pattern will yield very different attitudes toward consumption.

To address changes in consumer behavior successfully, companies must innovate, including a focus on value and an increased interest in health and wellness. Companies also should note the impact of rising digital connectivity—many French consumers, even as they age, will retain their attachments to communities and social networks. Indeed, we expect consumers aged 55 or older to account for 33 percent of the electronics market and 43 percent of the communications market in 2030, compared with 23 percent and 34 percent, respectively, in 2007.

Only a deep understanding of how category dynamics and consumer needs are changing will allow companies to weather the difficult market conditions in France and, more broadly, in Western Europe. Companies will need to adopt a granular approach that helps them target pockets of growth in a generally lackluster environment and anticipate changing consumer needs and behavior by adjusting their strategies and offerings. O

We welcome your comments on this article. Please send them to quarterly_comments@ mckinsey.com.

•   •   •

Equity analysts: Still too bullish

Marc H. Goedhart, Rishi Raj, and Abhishek Saxena

After almost a decade of stricter regulation, analysts' earnings forecasts continue to be excessively optimistic.

The earnings forecasts of stock analysts are an occupational hazard for CEOs and other C-suite executives. Those estimates are a benchmark of the current and future health of companies. But at the same time, they're often excessively optimistic—and a CEO who manages to their dictates risks destroying value if they shift attention from running existing businesses effectively to chasing transactions designed to boost earnings per share.

How far off are these forecasts? Nearly a decade ago, we took a close look at the accuracy of stock analysts' work, and the results were sobering. Analysts were overly bullish and slow to revise forecasts to reflect

Marc Goedhart is a consultant in McKinsey's Amsterdam office; Rishi Raj and Abhishek Saxena are consultants in the Delhi office.

Analysts' forecasts rarely hit the target, and the margin of error is large.

Earnings per share (EPS) for S&P 500 companies, $

—— Analysts' forecasts over time for each year   ● Realized EPS for each year

Date of forecast (Jan of each year)

Source: Thomson Reuters I/B/E/S Global Aggregates; McKinsey analysis

new economic conditions. We also found that forecast errors increased as economic growth declined. When we recently updated our analysis, we found that little had changed—despite new rules that regulators imposed, over the past decade, to improve the quality of analysts' forecasts, restore confidence in them, and prevent conflicts of interest.

The degree of the overshoot is large, averaging 100 percent over the past 25 years. Forecasts for earnings growth have hovered between 10 percent and 12 percent a year, while actual earnings growth averaged a more modest 6 percent. Meanwhile, exceptions to the long pattern of excessively upbeat forecasts are rare, as a progression of consensus earnings estimates for the S&P 500 clearly shows. Only in years such as 1988, 1994 though 1997, and 2003 through 2006, when economic growth was strong,

were analysts' long-term estimates at or below actual earnings.

Interestingly, the capital markets have a more realistic view of corporate performance (see exhibit below). Except during the market bubble of 1999–2001, actual P/E ratios have been 25 percent lower than implied price-to-earnings ratios based on analysts' forecasts. At present, for example, the actual forward P/E ratio of the S&P 500 is 14, which is consistent with long-term earnings growth of 5 percent. That's also more in line with our research indicating that long-term earnings growth for the market as a whole is unlikely to differ significantly from GDP growth.

In communicating with analysts, CEOs, CFOs, and other executives should be mindful of the excesses, of course. But we believe there are avenues of more productive engagement with the analyst com-

Capital markets often are closer to the mark in assessing company prospects.

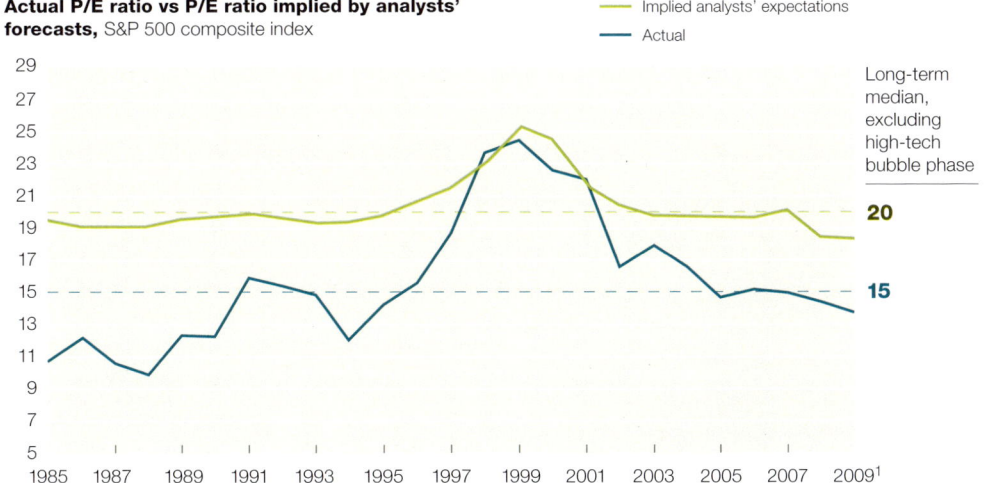

Actual P/E ratio vs P/E ratio implied by analysts' forecasts, S&P 500 composite index

— Implied analysts' expectations
— Actual

Long-term median, excluding high-tech bubble phase

20

15

[1] Based on data as of Nov 2009.

Source: Thomson Reuters I/B/E/S Global Aggregates; McKinsey analysis

munity. Many analysts have worked in major companies and possess broad industry experience. Their research reports often are comprehensive, grounded in discussions with multiple executives, and draw from a wide range of data sources. These reports may provide insights that complement or even run counter to what leaders are hearing from their own teams. This top-tier research, as well as interactions with the most widely respected analysts, can offer executives additional perspec-

tives and new data points when they set strategy. It is in those insights—much more than in the earnings forecasts accompanying them—that senior executives can find real value. o

We welcome your comments on this article. Please send them to quarterly_comments@ mckinsey.com.

Behind the findings

Analysts forecast growth of more than 10 percent for 70 percent of the S&P 500 companies we studied in our five-year earnings-growth analysis. Only in 1998–2001, when actual P/Es soared because of market bullishness, did the analysts' forecasts dip slightly below market sentiment.

To test the gap between forecast and actual earnings on a bigger sample size of companies, we also examined three-year earnings-growth estimates, based on analysts' year-on-year earnings estimates. The results were similar.

The full version of this article is available on mckinseyquarterly .com.

How basic behaviors drive sales success

Nate Boaz, John Murnane, and Kevin Nuffer

B2B customers say they care most about price, but what they really want is a great sales experience. For sales reps, that means getting the basics right.

When it comes to building valuable relationships with customers, sales representatives are critical players on the front lines. But are they getting the basics right? Customers want to be contacted just enough, not bombarded. Sales reps should know their products or services intimately and how their offering compares with those of their competitors. Customers need information on exactly how a product or service will make a difference to their businesses. And while they may say price is their biggest concern, a satisfying sales experience is ultimately more important.

These were the key findings of a survey we conducted of more than 1,200 purchasing decision makers in small, medium, and large companies throughout the United States and Western Europe who are responsible for buying high-tech products and services. The insights were consistent across simple to complex products and apply readily to most business-to-business (B2B) indus-

tries, which also have complex, multi–touch point sales processes involving both end users and purchasing professionals.

We found a big difference between what customers said was important and what actually drove their behavior. Customers insisted price was the dominant factor that influenced their opinion of a supplier's performance and, as a result, their purchasing decisions. Yet when we examined what actually determined how customers rated a vendor's overall performance, the most important factors were product or service features and the overall sales experience. The upside of getting these two elements right is significant: a primary supplier seen as having a high-performing sales force can boost its share of a customer's business by an average of 8 to 15 percentage points.

That makes the next finding all the more important. Of the many habits that undermine the sales experience,

Nate Boaz and John Murnane are associate principals in McKinsey's Atlanta office, where Kevin Nuffer is a consultant.

two that are relatively easy to fix accounted for 55 percent of the behavior customers described as "most destructive": failing to have adequate product knowledge and contacting customers too frequently. Only 3 percent said they weren't contacted enough, suggesting customers are open to fewer, more meaningful interactions.

Fortunately, both damaging habits can be fixed. Companies can address a lack of product knowledge by centralizing content development to guarantee a uniform message and creation of compelling value propositions for customers. And to ensure deep understanding, sales reps can receive experiential training and on-the-job coaching, preferably side by side with the content-development team. Finally, sales reps don't need

to know everything. When it comes to specifics, we found customers were more than happy to use self-serve or online tools and selectively tap specialist support for the most complex situations.

Striking the right balance between contacting customers too much and too little requires understanding their stated and actual needs. There should be a clear strategy for reaching out to customers based on needs and profit potential, with schedules dictating frequency. The best contact calendars center around events that create value for customers, such as semiannual business reviews, which provide an opportunity to assess customer needs and ensure satisfaction. The key is to recognize that customers are also looking to lower

Buyers cite two practices as most damaging to the customer relationship.

% of US and European customers selecting given selling activity as 'most destructive,'
Dec 2009, (n = 1,252)

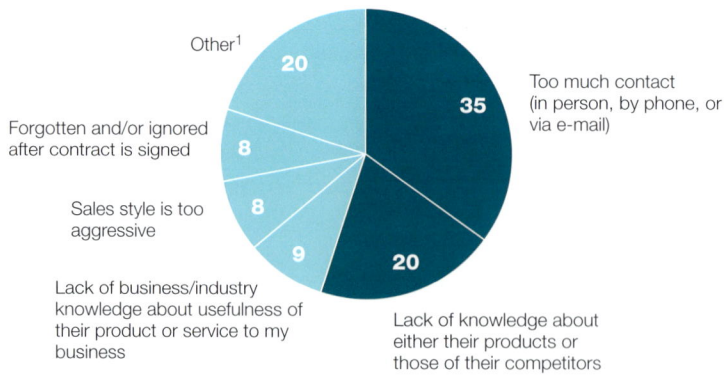

Other[1] — 20
Too much contact (in person, by phone, or via e-mail) — 35
Forgotten and/or ignored after contract is signed — 8
Sales style is too aggressive — 8
Lack of business/industry knowledge about usefulness of their product or service to my business — 9
Lack of knowledge about either their products or those of their competitors — 20

[1] Comprises the following issues, each cited by <6% of repondents: inconsistent sales team, slow response to sales-related inquiries, too little contact, no help in optimizing spending, no single point of contact available, no information sharing on matters specific to my business.

their interaction costs, so any contact with them must be meaningful.

The sales experience matters, and a good one starts by getting the basics right. Companies should examine exactly how they are performing by asking the following questions: What are the most influential drivers of the sales experience? What things are your sellers doing that could damage relationships? How does the perception your customers have of your sales force compare to how they view your competitors? It is only by knowing and understanding the answers to these questions that companies can begin to identify and pursue the right fixes. o

The authors would like to thank Eric Harmon and Maria Valdivieso de Uster for their contributions to this article.

Readers speak out

We invited mckinseyquarterly.com readers—customers and sales reps alike—to share their ideas on how sales reps might make interactions more meaningful.

Mary Jo Martin
President, Cynapsus, Houston, TX, USA

Negatives:
1. Sales reps who contact me by e-mail (when I have not given them permission) and use *bad* spelling and grammar

2. Sales reps who personalize e-mail, but get my name wrong

3. Sales reps who offer me products I have no use for

4. Sales reps who have next to no knowledge of my business

Positives:
1. Sales reps who try to develop a relationship with me

2. Sales reps who send me info that's useful for my business (without being "pushy")

Misty Khan
President, Advena Artemis, Houston, TX, USA

Early on in one of my first sales jobs, I asked one of my best customers if I could shadow him for a few hours during a time of day when he typically would use my product. I explained that I wanted to better understand how he was using the product and where it could be improved so that I could provide better support to him. He graciously invited me to spend half a day with him and took the time to explain how my product helped him do his job and where the weaknesses were. The experience was invaluable, and after ten years we still keep in contact.

Unlocking the elusive potential of social networks

Michael Zeisser

To realize the marketing potential of virtual activities, you have to make them truly useful for consumers.

There is much hype about social networks and their potential impact on marketing, so many companies are diligently establishing presences on Facebook, Twitter, and other platforms. Yet the true value of social networks remains unclear, and while common wisdom suggests that they should be tremendous enablers and amplifiers of word of mouth, few consumer companies have unlocked this potential. At Liberty Interactive, which comprises many specialty e-commerce companies, we wrestle daily with the question of how to realize the promise of social networks.

We do have pages on Facebook and active feeds on Twitter, but we never thought those steps alone would make a big difference to the performance of our companies. More recently, we have adopted a new mind-set: we think of word of mouth generated on social networks as a distinct form of media. This idea is more than a semantic detail. When you think of word of mouth as media, it becomes a form of content, and businesses can apply tried-and-true content-management practices and metrics to it. In addition, word of

mouth generated by social networks is a form of marketing that must be earned—unlike traditional advertising, which can be purchased. We therefore concluded that we could succeed only by being genuinely useful to the individuals who initiate or sustain virtual world-of-mouth conversations.

So what does it mean to be useful in a world of virtual conversations enabled by social networks? Obviously, there are no generic solutions, and each company will need to invent and discover what makes sense for its unique situation. We have, however, learned a few lessons that can be encapsulated in two primary insights. First, a powerful way for a brand to be useful in the virtual world is to confer social importance on its users. Second, "virtual items" are critical to stimulating social interactions that may in turn generate word of mouth.

The power of importance
An effective way for a brand to be useful in the context of social networks is to make people who originate a word-of-mouth con-

Michael Zeisser, an alumnus of Mckinsey's New York office, is a senior vice president at Liberty Media.

versation seem important within their own social environment. Recognition by peers is a powerful motivator, and brands that allow users to gain it deliver real perceived value. When users publicize that recognition, it translates into word of mouth. Companies can confer this kind of importance—for example, by issuing achievement "badges" that users can post to their Facebook profiles or by deploying leader boards or achievement scores of all types. As Web sites evolve to become increasingly dynamic experiences that let people interact in real time, the value to core users of being recognized for their prominence in a community will only increase.

We've also learned never to underestimate the value consumers place on opportunities to brag online about their achievements. That's made significantly easier through the clever integration of a Web site with Facebook and Twitter. We see this phenomenon daily—for example, on the forums of our Bodybuilding .com site. When members boast of reaching their target weight or other goals with help from Bodybuilding .com workouts, we receive authentic and credible word-of-mouth endorsements at almost no cost. In fact, if recent behavioral research is accurate, these experiences can create "contagions" in which the behavior of users is mirrored by their networks of friends, amplifying the word-of-mouth effect and reflecting well on the underlying brands.

The allure of virtual items

It's our strong intuition that virtual items play an important role in facilitating virtual word of mouth. This belief, at its core, is based on observing user behavior. While the notion of virtual goods—nonphysical objects used in online communities and games—still puzzles many executives, it's quite apparent that consumers love them. People acquire or compete for virtual items obsessively on Foursquare, Zynga, and many other sites. It is estimated that virtual goods have become a very real $5 billion industry worldwide.

So why do consumers pay real money for online objects that don't actually exist? Their motives reinforce our notion that users seek online importance: they purchase virtual goods primarily for self-expression (such as

As Web sites evolve to become increasingly dynamic experiences that let people interact in real time, the value to core users of being recognized for their prominence in a community will only increase.

virtual houses or virtual gifts) and for recognition (such as virtual badges for becoming, say, the "mayor" of a bar on Foursquare). These behaviors are too widespread and intense to be fads, and marketers need to recognize them as meaningful. Brands should actively experiment with ways to use virtual goods as catalysts of word-of-mouth media.

Virtual gifting is becoming an important consumer activity among Facebook members. Today, much of this activity is free, but Facebook is introducing a virtual-currency "credit" system that will allow sellers to get real dollars for their gifts and other items. In the context of a social network, it is not a stretch to conceive of virtual gifts as important objects, especially as their availability can be strictly limited. Just think about the fervor consumers accord collectibles of all kinds, from baseball cards to dolls to coins. If virtual items prove similarly desirable, they are likely to be a big deal for consumers and marketers, as well as a great tool to create useful word-of-mouth media.

We've also found that basic laws of consumer behavior still apply: consumers love a bargain, and companies should take full advantage of social networks as powerful notification tools. Users can be alerted to sales or to the expiration of a promotion, but companies must be mindful that these feeds and tweets are designed as catalysts to generate virtual word-of-mouth media. They are not social-media junk

mail, but legitimate content objects—actual pieces of media that we want the initial recipients to distribute to their friends.

One final recommendation: no gimmicks. Forget dancing monkeys, artificial contests, or stupid tricks; they add no value and waste people's time. A commitment to being useful in social-media activities means a commitment to creating only high-quality interactions. Again, regarding word of mouth as a media product makes it easier to define what quality means for your particular activities. There are clearly many ways for brands to make themselves useful to consumers, so managing virtual word of mouth goes well beyond maintaining a Facebook page or a Twitter account. Exactly how far remains to be seen, and companies should apply an experimental mind-set, while being careful not to overinvest.

Word-of-mouth marketing through social networks could emerge as an important tool in the marketer's arsenal. That will depend on whether marketers can tame the fundamentally unpredictable and serendipitous nature of word of mouth without losing what makes it so valuable in the first place—its authenticity. o

We welcome your comments on this article. Please send them to quarterly_comments@mckinsey.com.

On the cover

How to compete in a rebalancing global economy

Introduction

Peter Bisson, Elizabeth Stephenson, and S. Patrick Viguerie

The relentless rise of emerging markets is one of five fundamental forces reshaping the business landscape.

Peter Bisson is a director in McKinsey's Stamford office, Elizabeth Stephenson is a principal in the Chicago office, and Patrick Viguerie is a director in the Atlanta office.

Private equity is emblematic of an industry hit hard by the financial crisis. The overnight implosion of the M&A market and the simultaneous collapse of leveraged financing posed immediate and fundamental challenges to its business model. Yet, throughout the crisis, one thing didn't change at The Carlyle Group, a leading private-equity player headquartered in Washington, DC: its determination to continue seizing the opportunities arising from the ongoing, accelerating shift in global economic power from the developed to the developing world.

Five crucibles of change

1 The great rebalancing

Over the next decade, emerging markets will contribute more economic growth than will developed economies—for the first time in 200 years. This shift will spur a wave of innovation in product design, infrastructure, and value chains as local newcomers and established multinationals vie to serve hundreds of millions of new consumers at unimaginably low price points. Signs of breakthroughs to come: Tata's Nano (a $2,200 car), Godrej's ChotuKool (a $69 fridge that works without electricity), and GE's MAC 400 (an $800 electrocardiogram that's well suited to serve remote villages because it can conduct 100 tests on a single battery charge). Increasingly, such products can disrupt Western markets as well. Learning to win in low-cost, high-growth countries will be critical to winning everywhere else.

Percentage of executives who say this force ...	...is **important** for business	...will have a **positive effect** on profits	...is being **actively addressed** by their company
	85%	**48%**	**72%**

For more from executives on key global forces, see "Five forces reshaping the global economy: McKinsey Global Survey results," on mckinseyquarterly.com.

"Today," says David Rubenstein, Carlyle's cofounder and managing director, "we invest more money outside the US than in the US and have more people outside the US [doing that] investing than we have inside." Rubenstein is confident this trend will continue and points to Brazil, India, South Africa, Turkey, and, above all, China as countries that could make the transition from "emerging" to "great economic powers." Already, Carlyle employs 45 Chinese nationals in its operations there, and, tellingly, he adds, "Indigenous firms are now our biggest competitors in China."

To watch the full interview with David Rubenstein, visit mckinseyquarterly.com.

The message from Rubenstein and hundreds of other top executives McKinsey has spoken with over the past 18 months is clear: while the financial crisis and its aftershocks have understandably dominated

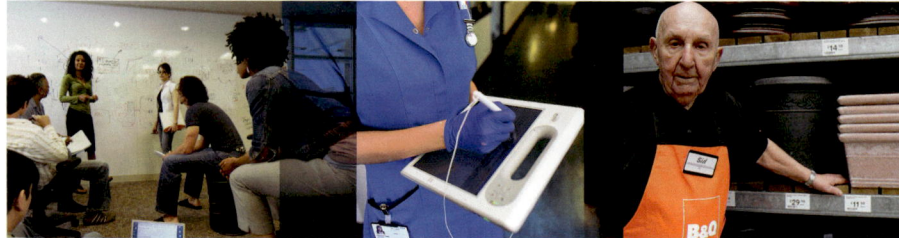

2 The productivity imperative

Weighed down by aging populations and slowing labor force growth, developed economies need extraordinary gains in productivity to enjoy continued growth. This requires reinventing government as well as inefficient industries such as health care. Finding marketable ways to "do it smarter" will be a huge growth opportunity. At every company, securing the right talent—and deploying tools such as machine-to-machine technologies, advanced analytics, and cloud computing to leverage knowledge workers—will be key sources of competitive advantage.

Percentage of executives who say this force ...	...is **important** for business	...will have a **positive effect** on profits	...is being **actively addressed** by their company
	57%	**40%**	**58%**

the news—and may for a while yet—the biggest mistake for business leaders would be to allow the short-term manifestations of the crisis to make those executives myopic. What really matters for most businesses is developing and executing the right strategies to deal with the longer-term implications of the great rebalancing of global economic activity that's underway.

In all likelihood, the next decade will mark the first since the Industrial Revolution when emerging economies contribute more to economic growth than all the developed countries combined. In the construction, agriculture, and mining sectors, this share of growth will be as high as 80 percent. GDP per capita will rise nearly five times faster in emerging economies than in OECD[1] nations. More people will escape poverty than during any other period in history. And by the end of the decade, roughly 40 percent of the world's population will have achieved middle-class status—up from less than 20 percent today.

[1] Organisation for Economic Co-operation and Development.

3 The global grid

A vastly more interconnected global economy, linked by rapid flows of capital, goods, and information, allows innovation to spread at unprecedented speed—but also spawns new and destabilizing cycles of volatility. Such a world puts a premium on resilience and rapid adaptation. The challenges and opportunities from this transformation will increase with the spread of mobile broadband—particularly in emerging markets. Just four in ten Kenyans have cell phones, yet half already use them to make purchases via mobile-payment systems. What's more, Kenya's largest employer is txteagle, a text-messaging company that doles out microwork to some 10,000 people.

Percentage of executives who say this force...	...is **important** for business	...will have a **positive effect** on profits	...is being **actively addressed** by their company
	61%	**41%**	**66%**

But this historic geoeconomic transformation is about much more than the birth of a huge new consumer market. As those formerly emerging markets expand, they will begin setting the direction of the global economy instead of largely reacting to events put in motion by wealthy Western countries. In addition to cementing their position as the world's factory, supplying low-cost goods and services, these economies will become major providers of capital and talent. Most important, they will drive innovation at scale as both local champions and established multinationals strive to reduce cost structures to a fraction of developed-world levels—while still delivering high-quality goods and services.

For much of the past year, McKinsey has been revisiting and testing assumptions about the key global forces that will shape the new era we are entering at breakneck speed. The conclusion from this work is that the areas to watch are those where the economy's future stresses and tensions are likely to be greatest—because they will also

4 Pricing the planet

Rising resource demand, increasingly constrained supplies, and a continued push for more environmental protection are on a collision course this decade. The clean-tech industry will boom, even as the world continues to run on carbon. A patchwork regulatory regime will offer a lot of opportunity for market arbitrage, while the probable lack of any global rule-setting should create a brisk business in environmental adaptation. For companies, boosting resource productivity will become even more essential. The global shipper UPS, for example, has already saved 2 percent on fuel costs by using software that plans delivery routes with fewer left turns.

Percentage of executives who say this force …	…is **important** for business	…will have a **positive effect** on profits	…is being **actively addressed** by their company
	48%	**23%**	**51%**

serve as the crucibles from which lasting change and innovation will arise. The five forces running along the bottom of this introduction emerged as the most important. To read a longer description of them, visit mckinseyquarterly.com.

The thinking presented there is, of necessity, exploratory rather than definitive. Precisely how these forces will play out and, as important, how they will interact is a story that's still unfolding. What we are confident of, as a result of intensive research, interview, and survey efforts, is that these are the topics that should be framing every organization's conversations about a future course and how best to shape it.

Over the next year, in the *Quarterly* and elsewhere, McKinsey will explore the business implications of each of these five forces. In this package, we focus on what is arguably the most profound of them: the extraordinary rise and vibrancy of emerging markets. In our latest

 5

The market state

Politicians are caught between the need to spur growth while also crafting stronger safety nets to shelter citizens from the strains of a globalizing world. These forces include higher structural unemployment in the West and rising income inequality everywhere. Despite widespread belief in the need to maintain open markets, the risk of populist backlash is high. How governments respond—and whether or not they make smart policy choices—may well be the biggest macrorisk of all. The most agile businesses will turn their ability to help solve the state's challenges into opportunity.

Percentage of executives who say this force ...	...is **important** for business	...will have a **positive effect** on profits	...is being **actively addressed** by their company
	57%	**39%**	**29%**

global survey of more than 1,400 executives, the growth of consumers in emerging markets topped the list of developments that respondents believe will prove to be most important for business over the next five years. One executive who's tuned into both the opportunity and the challenge presented by global economic rebalancing is Andrew Gould, CEO of oil-services giant Schlumberger. In a recent *Quarterly* interview, he marveled at the "incredible" productivity of a new software-development lab his company has opened in Beijing. "It's scary," he said. "It really is scary."

To watch the full interview with Andrew Gould, visit mckinseyquarterly.com.

Fewer than half of the executives we surveyed believe this trend will have a positive effect on their profits. But executives at Chinese and Indian companies report they are developing "new business models" at a significantly higher rate than companies in other regions say they are. In "Building a second home in China," authors Jeff Galvin, Jimmy Hexter, and Martin Hirt lay out what foreign multinationals need to do if they want to move to higher ground in the vital competitive battlefield that China has become.

The great rebalancing has its darker side as well. In our recent survey, 63 percent of respondents said they expect "increased overall volatility" to become a permanent feature of the global economy. In "Globalization's critical imbalances," Lowell Bryan offers some ideas about what executives can do to cope with the wide swings in commodity prices and currencies that seem sure to arise as the seemingly intractable global imbalances in trade and labor markets collide with the irresistible force of the great rebalancing. As companies seek to chart their own right path in this dynamic environment, the penalties for failing to adapt will be severe—and the rewards for genuine innovation extraordinary. o

Building a second home in China

Jeff Galvin, Jimmy Hexter, and Martin Hirt

Multinational companies hoping
to succeed in China can't treat it as an
interesting side bet any longer;
they need to take China as seriously
as they do their home market.

The problem

Few multinationals are committing to China a level of resources and management attention commensurate with the country's importance.

Why it matters

China is becoming the competitive battlefield where global winners are determined. Companies that succeed in China will create competitive advantages they can exploit in other markets. Companies that fail to do so may be vulnerable in their own home markets to attacks from Chinese companies and other multinationals that succeed in China.

What you should do about it

Even if you have been operating in China for years, challenge yourself to raise your organization's game in China by treating it as a second home. For example:

Rethink your aspirations for China with regard to market share, sourcing volumes, productivity, performance, and R&D activity.
Focus as much management attention on China as you do on your home market, including placing critical senior executives there.
Stop thinking about China as a market that's too nascent to require the same sophisticated approaches you employ elsewhere.
Instead, bring your best practices to China, in areas ranging from technology and product strategy to marketing, distribution, service, and supply chain management.

© Xiaoyang Liu/Corbis • Keren Su/Corbis

The past two years have underscored China's resilience and dynamism. Its economy has been booming against a backdrop of global stagnation. China's business environment, in particular, has been changing fast, with new regulatory policies and a rising cost of doing business affecting the playing field for multinationals (see sidebar "Cautious sentiments").

But the real story, in our view, isn't China's continued, rapid evolution. It's the fact that, in far too many cases, executives still aren't making China as central as it should be to their global strategy. In sectors ranging from auto parts to consumer electronics, semiconductors, aviation, and electricity transmission equipment, China is fast becoming the competitive battlefield on which global winners are determined. Even when companies are not competing in China, their Chinese and foreign rivals may soon be exploiting advantages earned there to compete in global markets.

With the stakes this high, the implication is clear: it is no longer possible for most companies to succeed in China while treating it merely as an interesting side bet. Instead, they need to start building a second home in China. At the core, this means committing a company as seriously to success in China as in its home market. The starting point is to set targets for performance in China that are on par with those at home: companies need to raise their aspirations for, and rigorously measure, a variety of targets. Some of them, such as senior-executive time spent on China and knowledge of Chinese customers, are challenging to quantify but no less important than more straightforward metrics regarding market share in China or sourcing volumes. Then companies need to deliver against those targets by bringing to China their global best practices across the value chain, adapting them as needed to local conditions, and executing against them. This sounds easy but happens so rarely that it's a powerful competitive differentiator.

Jeff Galvin is an associate principal in McKinsey's Shanghai office, Jimmy Hexter is a director in the Beijing office, and Martin Hirt is a director in the Taipei office.

Why you may need a second home in China

For a simple illustration of China's long-term importance, let's consider a relatively modest industry: piano manufacturing. By some estimates, China has at least 50 million piano students among its

650 million urban residents. As China adds 20 million urban residents every year and average incomes in cities rise, the number of piano students will surely grow in unison. It is not hard to imagine a time in the near future when China has 100 million piano students.

While the parents of these piano students will want to purchase pianos for their children, it is unlikely that the large and expensive pianos in many North American or European homes will be well-suited to smaller, multigenerational Chinese homes. Some company will develop and bring to market a value-priced, more appropriately sized piano that sells well in China. It may be Pearl River Piano; it may be Great Wall Instruments; it may be Steinway & Sons or

Cautious sentiments

An AmCham-China[1] survey published in March 2010 found that 38 percent of US businesses now feel foreign companies are "unwelcome" in China, up from 26 percent just two months earlier and the highest percentage recorded since AmCham began conducting the survey four years ago. The European Chamber of Commerce is reporting similar concerns among its members. The explanation for these cautious sentiments goes beyond recent tensions between China and Google or concerns about the value of the renminbi and China's role at the 2009 Climate Change Conference in Copenhagen.

For starters, there's a perception that efforts are under way to limit foreign companies' access to the Chinese market. In 2009, China announced a National Indigenous Innovation Product (NIIP) accreditation policy that would give advantage in government procurement to products certified as containing "indigenous innovation." Fifty-seven percent of foreign technology companies surveyed recently said the policy would hurt their future business, and 37 percent said they were already feeling the impact, even though the policy was not yet officially in place. Similarly, in 2009, a new antimonopoly law was created to prevent any company from gaining a dominant position that would affect the competitive landscape in China. The first use of this law was to block Coca-Cola's acquisition of China Huiyuan Juice.

What's more, the cost of doing business is rising. Wage growth has averaged 15 percent annually since 2000. The renminbi has risen, and most multinationals expect this trend to continue. Tax law changes in 2008 reduced certain investment incentives and imposed

Yamaha. Someone will do it. Once that company's piano wins in China and gains the advantages of scale, it will have a good chance of being successful, first, in other emerging markets (such as Brazil, India, and Turkey) and, soon thereafter, in Germany and the United States. While this may sound far-fetched, two-thirds of the world's violins are already made in China.

Pianos exemplify the impact China will have on the structure of many industries as its role in the global economy expands far beyond low-cost manufacturing. Now, in industries ranging from musical instruments to semiconductors to auto parts to electricity transmission equipment, competition in China is leading to the

a 10 percent withholding tax on repatriated dividends. All these factors reduce China's cost advantage versus other low-cost countries, while high stock market valuations of Chinese companies make it more expensive to grow through acquisitions.

Although we don't know how these trends will evolve, our experience—and the private reflections of executives who logged many miles in China—suggest that multinationals should take a long-term and comparative perspective on recent events. For example, some of the new tax rules represent, to a certain extent, a leveling of the playing field, which previously favored multinationals. Similarly, some new regulations, such as the antimonopoly law, have long-established analogues in the European Union and the United States and in fact represent China's own attempt to move toward developed-market norms. A top executive at one large multinational recently mused that many of China's policies today remind her of France's industrial policies 30 years ago—and German and US companies did not abandon the French market.

To repeat: there is a broad consensus that the introduction or application of new regulations appears to be disadvantaging some non-Chinese companies. But what seems equally clear is that China is going through an evolution in its business environment, and the end game is far from certain. Given the importance of the market, rather than turning away, prudence suggests looking hard for ways to navigate this dynamically evolving business landscape.

[1]The American Chamber of Commerce in the People's Republic of China.

creation of new products that have the potential to win in global markets—and, importantly, the winners can be either Chinese or foreign companies. One US company found that to be competitive in China, it had to redesign a semiconductor product to bring its cost down dramatically. Once the company was able to deliver such compelling value, its factory in China, which had been built to supply the domestic market, ended up exporting nearly 80 percent of its production.

In 2009, China became the world's largest market for cars. Here again, the initial game is local. But once the "value for money" cars now on sale in China reach a certain quality level, the global auto industry will likely be changed profoundly. It's only a matter of time: consider, for example, the relentless pursuit by Chinese companies of Western automotive assets—typified by Geely Automobile's recent acquisition of Volvo—and of capability-enhancing joint ventures, such as the two, involving Chinese companies and GM, that together expect to sell over two million vehicles this year. Meanwhile, BYD Auto, a Chinese battery maker that has been focusing on making an electric car, recently announced that it will have one for the US market in 2011. Warren Buffett is a believer: he bought a 10 percent stake for $230 million last fall.

Too few executives focus on China's long-term impact in a serious way—and when they do, most conclude that China is more important than they previously imagined.

Of course, it would be naïve to suggest that China must be a second home for every company or product line or that it will be possible in all cases to capture significant market share and scale advantages there and to exploit them globally. In some industries with dominant incumbent players or significant regulation (such as power generation or electricity transmission and distribution), it may not be feasible in the foreseeable future to gain significant Chinese market share.

Even where local market opportunities are limited, though, it's still possible to gain global advantages by leveraging China effectively. A company might, for example, develop a Chinese sourcing program that gives it a leg up on competitors in other markets by providing access to the lowest-price, high-quality components. Or it might establish a leading R&D center, become an extremely desirable employer, and leverage China's abundant pool of low-cost but high-quality engineering talent for global product development.

Determining the role and importance of China is an industry- and company-specific exercise that requires a combination of competitive analysis, market research, war-gaming, and creative scenario planning (for an example of forward-looking industry analysis in the Chinese automotive sector, see "Applying global trends: A look at China's auto industry," on page 115). In our experience, too few executives focus on China's long-term impact in a serious way—and when they do, most conclude that China is more important than they previously imagined.

Measuring your second home

We've written in the past about how Danfoss, a European industrial-controls manufacturer, overhauled its operations in China after deciding that a focus on market share, as opposed to revenue, was the only way to avoid being eclipsed by competitors.[1] Danfoss illustrates the importance of translating bold aspirations into metrics, which can be either quantitative or qualitative.

Quantitative metrics

Danfoss focused on market share, but that's just part of the equation. The key is to review the entire business model, understand where China's impact will be greatest, raise the relevant aspirations accordingly, and then measure them rigorously. For example, what percentage of a company's sourcing should come from China, and what should be the cost of the items sourced there? In our experience, when companies—whether they are retailers or electronic-component manufacturers—assess the economics of their Chinese suppliers as rigorously as they assess suppliers at home, they often find that

[1] See Jimmy Hexter and Jonathan R. Woetzel, "Bringing best practice to China," mckinseyquarterly.com, November 2007; and William E. Hoover Jr., "Making China your second home market: An interview with the CEO of Danfoss," mckinseyquarterly.com, February 2006.

It's not impossible for a US-based executive to develop the mind-set, gain the exposure, and stay sufficiently current on the Chinese market to make good, timely strategic and operational decisions.

despite how low procurement costs in China seem, they still are overpaying significantly by local standards. Manufacturing productivity is another area worth measuring seriously. In many industries, Chinese factories today can achieve the same levels of productivity as those elsewhere in the world. Or consider this: how many PhDs in Xi'an might be worth hiring to support global product-development efforts?

All that said, market share is not a bad starting point for many companies. Conducting "how big could we really become?" exercises can be eye opening. For example:

Medical equipment. One medical-equipment company found that the potential market in China for its products was 35 percent larger than it had thought, simply because it had not previously considered a large group of customers whose budgets, it wrongly perceived, were too small to be worth targeting.

Infrastructure. An infrastructure company found that the market for its existing products was 140 percent larger than it previously estimated, largely because it had been considering only the same industrial-customer segments it served outside of China.

Industrial automation. An industrial-automation company found that the premium segments it had initially targeted constituted just 25 to 35 percent of the potential market opportunity for its products. And while the gross margins in the segments it served were indeed higher (around 40 to 50 percent), those in the value segment it was neglecting were still 25 to 35 percent, on average.

Qualitative metrics

Alongside such quantitative metrics, companies seeking to build a second home in China need to pay at least as much attention to softer measures of their commitment to the country. Surprisingly, many European and US executives who ask themselves questions like the ones below identify a significant gap between the stated importance of China and its actual place on their priority lists:

Time spent in China. How much time each year do your global CEO, CFO, and other C-suite executives actually spend in China? When was the last time the company held a board meeting in China? How does this compare with the number of trips or board meetings in Europe, Latin America, or North America? Is this the right balance?

Visibility into China operations. Do any of your China business leaders, within either corporate functions or business units, report directly to the CEO? Is the person reporting to the CEO about China based there? Are your China operations important enough to your company's future that the CEO should hear about them firsthand?

Chinese representation in the senior team. How many of the company's board members are from China? How many top executives are from China?

Knowledge of Chinese customers and suppliers. In the home market, most CEOs and business unit leaders know the CEOs of current (and potential) customers and suppliers quite well. Does your CEO have similar personal relationships in China?

Relationships with government leaders and regulators. In home markets, top business leaders know government leaders and regulators well and often join government advisory boards. Does your CEO have the same level of familiarity with government leaders and regulators overseeing your business in China? Do you play any advisory roles in China that are similar to those you play in your home market?

One multinational was so disturbed by its answers to questions like these that it immediately promoted the leaders of its major business units in China to the same executive status as the leaders of businesses in Western Europe. Another company, after investigating why it had identified many promising acquisition targets in China yet never followed through on them, found that nearly all of the acquisition ideas were being vetoed within its business units before reaching the CEO. In response, the CEO created a monthly China M&A review.

These examples highlight an organizational issue. Many multinationals have a "China CEO" who is the public face of the company there and tries to develop or influence overall China strategy. But line operations in China often roll up into global business units or functions headquartered in Europe, Japan, or the United States, where most of the P&L responsibility typically remains. The home market also continues to "own" and make decisions for global R&D, product development, IT, and other functions. In this way, business unit leaders in China effectively become sales managers—several steps removed from real decision making about what they are selling and sometimes even how they are selling it.

© Bloomberg/Getty Images

It's not impossible for a US-based executive to develop the mind-set, gain the exposure, and stay sufficiently current on the Chinese market to make good, timely strategic and operational decisions. But it's hard—which is why we believe more companies will need to place significant global leaders in China, as Wal-Mart Stores did several years ago when it moved to Shenzhen the company's head of sourcing, who has made major contributions to Wal-Mart's Chinese sourcing efforts. IBM, too, recently moved its global sourcing leader to China. (See sidebar "How one company is making China its first home" for another example.)

Making your second home as strong as your first

While it may sound obvious that companies should bring their best practices to China, too often that's the exception rather than the rule. Few multinationals conduct anywhere close to the same level of primary customer research in China as they would in Europe or the United States. Many distribution systems have insufficient reach or are outsourced to third parties purely on the basis of cost or ease of setup. After-sales service is rarely as good in China as it would

(continued on page 52)

We believe more companies will need to place significant global leaders in China, as Wal-Mart Stores did several years ago when it moved to Shenzhen the company's head of sourcing, who has made major contributions to Wal-Mart's Chinese sourcing efforts.

How one company is making China its first home

Julian Birkinshaw

Irdeto Access, a Dutch software company, recently moved its CEO and global headquarters to China. In 2007, the producer of content security solutions for media operators in digital pay-TV, Internet, and mobile communications was a 700-employee company headquartered in Amsterdam. Most of its sales had historically been in Europe, but the growth opportunities were primarily in Asia. As CEO Graham Kill recalled, "A mother ship in Holland, with satellite regions elsewhere, was not going to provide us with the growth we wanted." Nor did Kill feel "well placed to respond" to Chinese competitors, such as China Digital TV, that "had emerged from nowhere and were eroding our positions."

After considering a number of options, the company decided to replace its Amsterdam headquarters with a "dual-core" headquarters split between Amsterdam and Beijing. This meant that decision making and traditional headquarters functions would be shared across the two locations. To show commitment to the change, Kill moved himself and his family to Beijing in August 2007, with two other members of the executive team following in 2008. Over the next two years, Irdeto's business in Asia grew dramatically, and many customers pointed to the CEO's Beijing location as a factor in their decision to work with the company.

The new arrangements also led to measurable changes in internal attitudes and behavior. Irdeto allowed me to survey managers prior to the December 2007 headquarters shift, and then twice afterward, in 2008 and 2009. Among other things, I looked, using network analysis,[1] for changes in the degree to which middle managers based in Asia found themselves centrally involved in and able to influence decision-making processes. The change was dramatic: the centrality of Asian (not just Chinese) managers rose more than 20 percent, and their level of influence increased nearly 30 percent. By the time of the 2009 survey, in fact, the influence scores for Asian managers actually exceeded those for Europeans (exhibit). The quality and quantity of communication between the Asian and European parts of the company also improved significantly.

[1]For more on network analysis, see Robert L. Cross, Roger D. Martin, and Leigh M. Weiss, "Mapping the value of employee collaboration," mckinseyquarterly.com, August 2006; and Robert L. Cross, Salvatore Parise, and Leigh M. Weiss, "The role of networks in organizational change," mckinseyquarterly.com, April 2007.

Of course, Irdeto faces some practical challenges in making its dual-core headquarters work. Not every senior executive is prepared to sign up for a spell in Beijing, and executive-committee meetings are harder to schedule than they used to be. But for Graham Kill, these are problems the company simply needs to work through. And as more Asian executives move into senior-management positions, the model becomes easier to sustain.

After Irdeto shifted to dual-core headquarters with locations in Amsterdam and Beijing, the centrality and influence of its managers in Asia rose dramatically.

Network analysis of centrality and influence
(based on surveys of ~50 senior and middle managers at Irdeto
with response rate of ~80%)

	Degree of centrality[1] (higher score = greater average centrality of managers)		Index of overall influence[2] (higher score = more influence)	
	Asian managers	**European managers**	**Asian managers**	**European managers**
2007	29.2	36.5	0.87	1.15
Shift to dual-core headquarters in Dec 2007				
2008	35.0	43.8	0.94	1.09
2009	35.4	45.8	1.12	1.10

[1] Degree to which managers reported being centrally involved in decision-making processes; highest possible score cannot exceed number of managers in network.
[2] Degree to which managers reported being able to influence decision-making processes; the measure indicates the influence of the regional office over global strategy, with an average score of 1.

Source: Julian Birkinshaw

Julian Birkinshaw is a professor at the London Business School.

be in a multinational's home market. The same often goes for manu-facturing and product development.

One common rationale is that China is insufficiently developed to require the same sophisticated approaches employed elsewhere. Another is that despite China's potential, the current market size makes investments in, say, cutting-edge market research or after-sales service uneconomic. Both views are shortsighted at best. Yes, the functional capabilities of most multinationals outshine those of many Chinese competitors. But the Chinese are catching up fast, and other multinationals are also in the mix. Those who wait for others to develop the market may well find that the game is over by the time they decide to give it their best shot.

Below are examples of simple steps that multinationals are taking to bring their natural strengths to bear in four key areas—technology and product strategy, marketing, distribution and service, and supply chain management. These areas, along with human resources and government relations, are all ripe with opportunity for multi-nationals to differentiate themselves (see sidebar "Is your second home as strong as your first?" for a set of diagnostic questions for multi-nationals about each area).

Technology and product strategy

In many, though certainly not all, product categories, Western and Japanese firms still have technology advantages over local Chinese rivals. What's more, our research and experience with Chinese con-sumers, as well as corporate and government customers, reveal a will-ingness among some segments—even value-oriented ones—to pay a premium for higher-quality products. Making the right trade-offs between product benefits and pricing levels often requires break-ing with a company's single Europe- or US-centered product strategy.

For example, a leading global infrastructure company was frustrated by its inability to win large tenders in China, despite having the best technology and a lower operating cost over time than domestic or international rivals. Interviews with the infrastructure com-pany's customers revealed, however, that their procurement processes promoted lower capital expenditures; total cost of ownership was a minor consideration. In response, the company decided to go to mar-ket with two products: the existing, top-of-the-line imported one, which would remain appealing to a subset of customers, and a new value-oriented product featuring technology that was better than any rival could offer but manufactured in China and priced similarly to products from the company's Chinese rivals. This simple, segmented approach to product design, based on straightforward customer research, is something the multinational probably would have adopted long ago if conditions in the EU countries or the United States had demanded it. But with managers in the United States still making product decisions, the opportunity had been missed in China—until the company began paying that market more attention.

Our research and experience with Chinese consumers, as well as corporate and government customers, reveal a willingness among some segments to pay a premium for higher-quality products.

Marketing

Marketing, as practiced by leading Western companies, is a nascent concept in China. Most Chinese companies develop products for the local market primarily on the basis of an intuitive, experience-based understanding of customer needs. Market research, when undertaken, rarely probes for the sort of nuanced understanding that fuels product innovation in developed markets. Coca-Cola, Colgate-Palmolive, P&G, and other global packaged-goods players are competing effectively in many categories by exploiting their sophistication in market research, product development, and brand management. In contrast, few Chinese companies have significant experience to date developing sophisticated brand messages or images.

Nonetheless, in our experience, many multinationals—even leading ones—make mistakes, such as segmenting the Chinese market as they would developed markets, and are astounded at how far off base their underlying assumptions prove to be when they actually

conduct deep customer research. For example, when one large consumer goods company applied sophisticated customer research
techniques to its distribution strategy for a new product, it completely
revamped its rollout plan. Instead of prioritizing high-end customers
in widely dispersed large and wealthy cities, it switched to a more
targeted approach that focused on customers who exhibited similar
preferences but lived in smaller city "clusters" within close proxi-
mity. The benefits were twofold: first, these customers were more
receptive, on average, to the brand; and, second, the regional
approach made it much easier for the company to ensure consistent,
high-quality distribution from a single partner in each locality.

Distribution and service

In a country with as many dispersed and hard-to-reach markets as
China, third-party distributors are sometimes necessary. But
multinationals relying on them need to make sure these distributors
don't underinvest in service levels and quality—which is a common
practice for Chinese companies. In an attempt to grow rapidly and
at low investment levels, one multinational chose to distribute its
products through poorly trained third-party distributors that sold
them, alongside rivals' offerings, on a price-per-kilogram basis.
The company, frustrated with its performance—running a distant
second to the leading multinational player in the market, with
Chinese peers rapidly catching up—began creating a large direct-
sales force trained to help solve customers' problems. For other
companies, distributors may still be the right answer, provided that
it's possible to craft a partnership that can tailor sales and service
to customer needs.

Supply chain management

In recent years, as sales volumes in China and volatility have
increased for multinationals, many have found that their traditional
practice—retaining core planning functions at a global headquarters while relying on simple production and shipping requests
to guide Chinese supply operations—no longer works. One leading
electronics multinational watched inventories explode as planners
found it impossible to coordinate production flows. The company
first moved three experienced executives to China to stabilize the
situation and then began reorganizing its global-planning roles,
boosting the number and skill level of local planners and investing

Is your second home as strong as your first?

Technology and product strategy	Do you offer as large a range of products in China as you do in your home market? Have these products been designed based on Chinese customers' needs, or are they simply imported or "de-featured" Western designs? Are your price points at the same level as similar offerings from local or even foreign competitors?
Marketing	Has your company invested to know your customers in China as well as you do those in your home market? Is your market intelligence team in China just as big as the one your home market? Do you conduct as many primary market research studies as you do in your home market? Is your customer segmentation just as rigorous—or have you just applied one you use elsewhere?
Operations	Do you expect the same operational-performance levels in China as you do in your home market? Have you invested as many resources or as much expertise in building and refining your Chinese manufacturing, distribution, supply chain, and service models as you have in the European Union and the United States? Are your customer service centers just as close to Chinese customers as your centers in your home market are to customers there? Or have you taken shortcuts because "China is different"—such as working through third-party distributors, though you go direct everywhere else in the world?
Human resources	Is your HR team in China on the same scale as the one in the European Union or the United States? Do you follow a similarly rigorous process for finding potential hires—or do you rely more on references? Do you invest just as much in professional training and development programs, taught by equally qualified staff, as you do in your home market? Do you offer the same type of global rotational programs to rising Chinese executives as you do to those in other markets? Is your CEO just as aware of a rising star in the Shenzhen office as he is of someone in St. Louis or Munich?
Government relations	Do you have just as many and as capable government relations staff in China as you do in your home market? Do you have a similarly well-thought-through process for communicating with your regulators at the central, provincial, and city levels in China as you would in other markets? Are you helping to shape regulations there in the same way as you would elsewhere?

in more advanced IT support systems. These efforts to bring the Chinese supply chain up to global standards have been so successful that the company is revamping its entire supply chain across 14 of its Chinese factories and 30-odd external vendors.

•   •   •

China is becoming the world's most important competitive battlefield, with companies that succeed there creating a foundation for global leadership. Multinationals hoping to win this game must recognize that China needs to be much more than a significant growth market; it needs to become their second home. ○

Globalization's critical imbalances

Lowell Bryan

Future financial crises could accelerate the rebalancing of global economic activity from developed to emerging markets. The strategic implications— which touch on everything from companies' manufacturing footprints to the customers they target to how they structure their balance sheets— are profound.

The problem
Labor can't be freely traded on a single global market, but capital and commodities can. This dynamic is creating significant tensions in global currency, commodity, and debt markets.

Why it matters
The release of those tensions will have profound strategic implications. For example, the dollar and euro would need to be devalued by 30 to 50 percent for the purchasing-power-parity exchange rate of emerging-market currencies to reflect financial foreign-exchange rates more closely. Such a shift would dramatically affect the attractiveness of running operations and serving customers in different countries.

What you should do about it
Don't assume prevailing globalization norms will continue. Prepare for future financial shocks, partly through scenario planning around rapid currency or commodity price shifts. Also, prepare for a time when emerging markets are at least as important as drivers of consumption as they are platforms for low-cost operations.

To some extent, the rebalancing of global economic activity from developed to emerging markets simply reflects economic laws of gravity. In a world where ideas can flow freely and countries are at different stages in adopting modern modes of production, communication, and distribution, less developed nations should grow more rapidly than their counterparts in the West as they catch up.

But it's also important to understand that emerging-market economies have a structural advantage that is grounded in the operation of the global economy. Saber-rattling Western trade negotiators frequently focus their attention on the "unnaturally" depressed exchange rates of countries such as China, and this is a component of the structural advantage to which I refer. But its roots run far deeper—all the way down to the fundamental issue that labor can't be freely traded on a single global market, while capital and commodities can. Any company sourcing its production or service operations in a lower-wage emerging-market country therefore can save enormously on labor costs. That's painful for displaced Western workers, but it's good for the company's profits, good for consumers in developed markets, and good for the newly minted citizens of the global economy who are working in emerging-market factories and call centers. This is a dynamic we take so much for granted that it's easy to imagine it as a semipermanent condition that will underpin global economic development for the foreseeable future.

But what if it weren't? This article explains why we should consider that seeming improbability and examines the possibility that financial crises may accelerate the transition to a global economy with more balanced trade, capital flows, and consumption. I believe senior executives need to prepare now for a world that—as China's recent decision to relax its informal peg of the yuan to the US dollar underscores—*will* be coming to grips with an unsustainable set of economic relationships. Their unwinding will have serious long-term implications for those executives' strategic priorities, including where they locate operations and what customers they serve in which markets. Equally important is the need for preparedness in case the unwinding process is sudden and abrupt. While we surely seem to be headed toward a new global equilibrium, the transition to that future world may not be smooth and gradual.

Lowell Bryan is a director in McKinsey's New York office.

Adam Smith meets the global economy

We usually think of the global economy in terms of outputs such as cars and packaged goods. Yet the real integration of the world's economy begins with factors of production. Of those, commodities, capital, and labor are the most important for understanding our structural economic issues. The test of whether a market has fully formed is whether all customers get the same items at the same price, allowing for transaction and transportation costs. (This condition, called the law of one price, was originally advanced by Adam Smith.) Such market conditions have long existed at a global level for natural commodities, such as crude oil, bauxite, and iron ore, as well as for manufactured commodities, such as petroleum, aluminum, and steel. The law of one price also exists for freely traded foreign exchange and most instruments traded in the capital market. It does not exist for labor, however—which is the fundamental structural issue the global economy faces.

To understand labor's role, of course, you need to understand arbitrage. Cross-border arbitrage in the financial economy focuses on tradable instruments denominated in various currencies. In the real economy, such arbitrage focuses on capturing differences in the cost of production across geographies. As markets have opened and transaction and transportation costs fallen over the past quarter century, arbitrage opportunities in global financial markets and commodities have been quickly exhausted, so they easily meet the global law-of-one-price test. Yet there are still enormous arbitrage opportunities available in labor rates: the cost of performing the same job in different nations can vary significantly. As a result, multinational corporations that are able to source their production in emerging markets can enjoy large labor cost savings.

Until recently, labor arbitrage across countries was hard to capture because high-quality, highly productive labor was scarce in emerging markets. In the past decade, however, it has become relatively easy for companies to capture such opportunities, thanks to the combination of urbanization, education, infrastructure investments, new technology, the spread of advanced production techniques, and the evolution of digital standards. Even today, the cost of labor in China or India is still only a fraction (often less than a third) of the equivalent labor in the developed world. Yet the productivity of Chinese and Indian labor is rising rapidly and, in specialized areas (such as high-tech assembly in China or software development in

India), may equal or exceed the productivity of workers in wealthier nations. Given such differences, more and more companies around the world are locating production in emerging markets.

Labor costs and currencies

The structural issue facing developed-world nations is that the amount of high-quality, high-productivity labor that will be mobilized over the next decade in Brazil, China, and India (not to mention Mexico, the Philippines, and Thailand) is likely to be measured in the hundreds of millions of people. By comparison, the entire US labor force comprises 150 million people. This is a wonderful trend for humankind and would be a boon for everyone in the world if emerging-market employment were directed largely toward production for domestic consumption. The challenge for developed-world governments and citizens seeking jobs, however, is that a significant fraction of this emerging-world labor displaces jobs that would otherwise be created in Europe, Japan, and the United States. This may be the underlying reason why unemployment in Europe,

The job losses of the Great Recession follow a pattern different from that of previous recessions and may reflect structural, rather than cyclical, causes.

US employment during recessions[1]

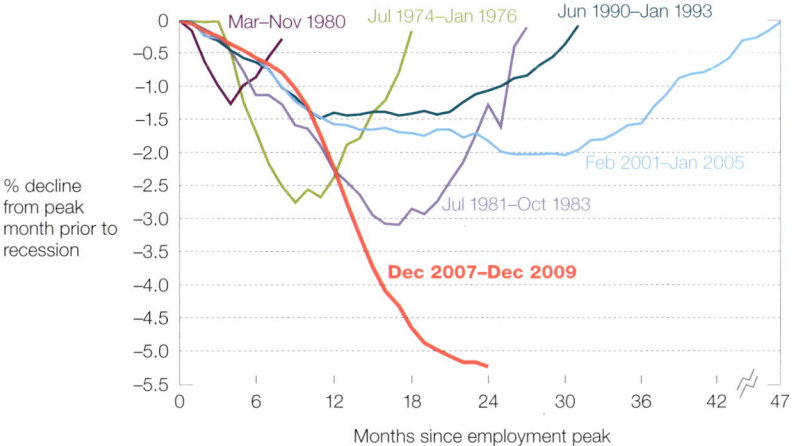

Months since employment peak

[1] Total nonfarm employment, seasonally adjusted.

Source: US Bureau of Labor Statistics

Japan, and the United States is becoming more structural rather than cyclical and may get worse over time no matter how much public stimulus is provided. Certainly, the job losses of the Great Recession look quite different from those of past recessions.[1]

In a completely open global capital market, foreign-exchange rates would adjust until labor markets in the developed world began to be competitive again, even if it took a major currency revaluation to achieve competitive parity. However, exchange rates in countries such as India and China have often been subject to foreign-exchange controls and interventions of various kinds. The result is that exchange rates haven't adjusted freely, leading to the shifting of developed-world service jobs offshore (particularly to India) and the migration of manufacturing jobs (particularly to China).

Assume, for the moment, that Europe, Japan, and the United States continue to run structural fiscal deficits and relatively loose monetary policies and to struggle with job creation. Also assume that China's recent announcement of a return to the "managed floating exchange rate" that prevailed from 2005 to 2008 does not mark the end of currency market interventions by emerging-market nations. Both scenarios are likely, so tensions between developed-world currencies and emerging-market currencies will probably continue to build. In particular, as more and more emerging-market citizens capture job opportunities associated with production and services for developed-world nations, the structural pressures on advanced countries will continue to increase. For example, it's hard to see how the United States can resume the rapid GDP growth necessary to reduce its fiscal deficit—which requires increased tax revenue and lower government spending—when almost 20 percent of its working population is unemployed or underemployed.

As the GDP growth of emerging-market nations continues to outstrip that of the developed world, the pressure on currency values will continue to build. Eventually, the tension must be released, and currency values will readjust. For all of us, the speed of that adjustment makes a big difference. The dollar and euro would need to be devalued by between 30 and 50 percent for financial foreign-exchange rates to reflect the purchasing-power-parity (PPP) exchange rates of emerging-market currencies more closely (and, therefore, for labor of equal quality and productivity to be priced relatively equally across geographies). An adjustment of this

---

[1] For a perspective on the relationship between offshoring and employment from 2000 to 2003, see Martin Neil Baily and Robert Z. Lawrence, "Don't blame trade for US job losses," mckinseyquarterly.com, February 2005.

magnitude that took just a few weeks, rather than a few years, would obviously jolt the global economy.

Commodity complications

Commodities are a further complication. Ramping up production in China, India, and other countries to capture the economic returns from the increasing supply of high-quality, productive labor requires more commodities to produce more output. Since the global law of one price applies to commodities, this means that, with all else held equal, producers in China and India end up paying more than they would if those countries' currencies were stronger. Simply put, commodity prices are too high in emerging-market countries and too low in developed-world countries.

As a result, developed-world consumers are using more commodities than they should, while emerging-market consumers are using fewer than they otherwise would. That's distorting pricing feedback to customers and suppliers. What's more, some of the returns that companies theoretically should be earning by taking advantage of low-cost, high-quality, productive labor in emerging markets is instead transferred to commodity-exporting nations. The resulting surpluses often then wind up in sovereign-wealth funds for deployment in the global capital market.

The fact that commodity prices, to a greater extent than currency values, are set in truly global markets where nations have little power over prices suggests that financial tensions will build earlier,

It's hard to see how the United States can resume the rapid GDP growth necessary to reduce its fiscal deficit when almost 20 percent of its working population is unemployed or underemployed.

Food prices have been extremely volatile since 2006 and are on the rise again.

FAO Food Price Index, monthly change in international prices of a basket of food commodities, Jan 2000–Mar 2010

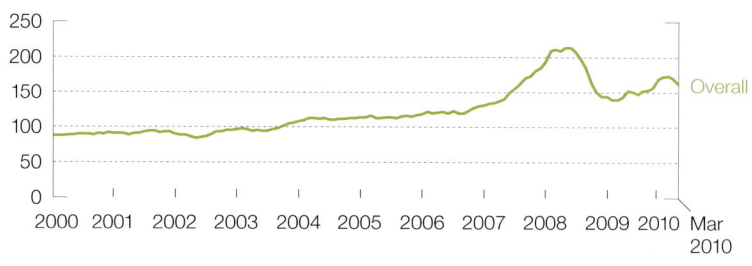

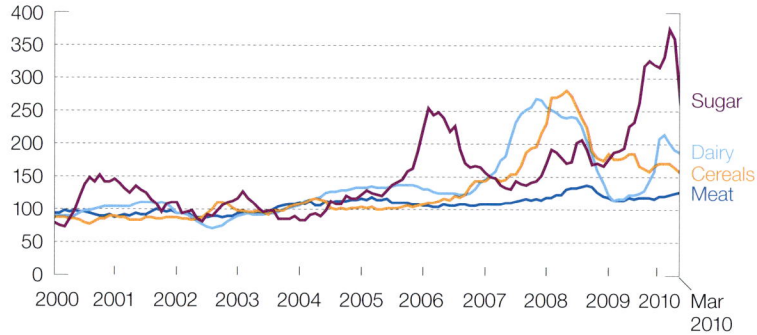

Source: Food and Agriculture Organization of the United Nations

and with greater volatility, in commodity than in currency markets. Some argue, in fact, that the last crisis was precipitated by the unbelievably rapid commodity price rise, in mid-2008, that saw oil jump to $140 a barrel, from $60 in early 2007, and coal increase to $170 a metric ton, from $50, over the same period. There are already signs that commodity prices are coming under pressure, even though developed-world growth remains relatively stagnant. Most commodity prices have doubled from their 2009 lows. Perhaps most disquieting, food prices have risen rapidly. It seems quite plausible that we could have a repeat of the commodity price movements of 2008 in late 2010 and 2011, even if developed-world GDP growth is only modest.

A dramatic increase in commodity prices could stall global economic recovery and also be the catalyst for emerging markets to revalue their currencies upward against the dollar and euro to reduce the high cost of imported commodities. Even the prospect of such a revaluation could cause large dollar and euro asset holders, such as sovereign-wealth funds, to accelerate the diversification of their holdings away from those currencies into foreign direct investment in emerging markets. That, in turn, could help trigger a currency crisis.

Adjustment uncertainty

It is very difficult to say how these issues will play out. The global rebalancing that is needed is obvious: developed-world countries need to save more, consume less, become more fiscally disciplined, and run current-account surpluses (or at least be neutral). Emerging-world countries need to let their currencies rise until PPP rates are closer to financial-exchange rates. They need to consume more, save less, run current-account deficits (or at least be neutral), and continue investing, with some of the capital provided by outsiders. If major national governments work proactively together to rebalance and coordinate their fiscal, monetary, trade, and foreign-exchange policies, the adjustment process could be gradual.

But such a policy adjustment is easier said than done. Developed-world politicians must respond to the demands of voters who don't understand how the global economy works or what has changed in recent years and who mostly want policies that are fiscally unbalanced. They generally want governments to spend more money on social programs—in the United States, for example, on Social Security and Medicare—without increasing taxes to pay for that additional spending. The usual response by developed-world governments to such dilemmas is to run bigger fiscal deficits and to borrow more money. Yet most developed-world governments have been rapidly exhausting their debt capacity, and some nations, such as Greece, Portugal, and Spain, are already experiencing fiscal crises. At some point, the International Monetary Fund and major nations could become unable, or unwilling, to bail out overly indebted governments, at which point defaults and debt restructurings would become inevitable.

Emerging-market leaders have different challenges. In general, they have been "virtuous": most have low debt-to-GDP ratios, maintain large currency reserves, continue to run current-account surpluses, and provide more capital to the developed world than they receive. Their economies are based upon undervalued currencies, low-cost labor, high savings rates, exports, and investment in infrastructure. These countries are wary of growing too rapidly or

The underlying global economic processes under way are very powerful, and the profit opportunities will be enormous as four billion people in emerging markets triple or quadruple their incomes and wealth over the next 20 years.

allowing too great a volume of capital inflows, particularly since, with undervalued currencies, they don't want to sell their assets cheaply. They also are wary of anything that would derail their growth, given the rising expectations of their populations.

Both sides, of course, need to give way. In the longer term, the capital markets will discipline governments if the imbalances—particularly the fiscal imbalances of developed-world governments—continue to grow. But in the short term, the powerful market states involved (for instance, the United States, the eurozone countries, Japan, China, India, Brazil, and major commodity-exporting nations) are so large and can pull so many levers that they exercise significant power in the global capital market, resisting its discipline. If that's the path they choose, it's likely that the tensions created by unbalanced and divergent policies will build until they cause rapid currency shifts, massive changes in commodity prices, and punitive interest rate increases (or even defaults) for overly indebted sovereign borrowers.

The corporate agenda

Companies have much more freedom in the global economy than governments do. They can more easily capture the opportunities created by divergent, unbalanced government policies. They can position themselves to capture profits from both cross-geographic labor arbitrage and the consumption growth that results from rising incomes in emerging markets. They also have significant opportunities to serve the changing needs of aging populations in the developed world.[2] The underlying global economic processes

[2] See David Court, "Serving aging baby boomers," mckinseyquarterly.com, November 2007.

under way are very powerful, and the profit opportunities will be enormous as four billion people in emerging markets triple or quadruple their incomes and wealth over the next 20 years.

That said, business leaders should not be sanguine about what lies in store. Although it's impossible to know in advance the speed or intensity of the needed adjustment, turmoil probably lies ahead. Here are four suggestions for executives hoping to get out in front of it:

> For starters, as companies plot their global footprints, executives should not assume that the prevailing reality of globalization will continue. Labor arbitrage opportunities won't disappear, of course, but strategies predicated on them could become less remunerative—maybe gradually or perhaps all at once.

> Second, it would be wise to be prepared for the high probability of future financial shocks. To do so, most companies need to become more adept at risk management and to err on the side of being overcapitalized, overliquid, and overprepared.

> Third, companies should engage in serious scenario planning around "unthinkables." These might include the potential for significant, rapid shifts in currency values (for example, a 30 percent decline of the dollar versus emerging-market currencies); an exit from the euro by some nations; dramatic, rapid changes in commodity prices (for example, oil prices spiking to $200 a barrel); or defaults on debt by major nations.

> Finally, multinational-company executives who set strategy in emerging markets need to stop *saying* that those markets may someday be at least as important as drivers of consumption as they are platforms for low-cost manufacturing or services—and to start *acting* as if that day was near. In an accompanying article, my colleagues Jeff Galvin, Jimmy Hexter, and Martin Hirt describe what it would mean for a multinational to treat China as its "second home" (see "Building a second home in China," on page 39). China's scale makes its potential to transform the competitive balance of industries, and thus its importance, somewhat unique. But as currency adjustments bring purchasing power closer to parity around the world, the importance of emerging-market consumption will be reinforced everywhere. (For more on consumer segments in those markets, see "Capturing the world's emerging middle class," on page 12.)

These suggestions represent specific applications of the more
dynamic management approach I have urged companies to adopt
in the past. The hallmarks of that approach—heightened aware-
ness, greater resilience, more flexibility, and the timely alignment
of leadership around needed adjustments—will be invaluable for
companies as they navigate the choppy waters of global economic
rebalancing. This process will continue and perhaps even accelerate in the years ahead, not despite, but because of the structural
adjustments that are needed to put the global economy on a
more sustainable trajectory. o

For more on how companies can best
respond to volatile conditions, see "Dynamic
management: Better decisions in
uncertain times," on mckinseyquarterly.com.

© Paul Hardy/Corbis • Jon Hicks/Corbis

Spotlight on CEO transitions

The problem
How should a new CEO use his or her time during the early days on the job?

Why it matters
Experienced CEOs say if new leaders fail to make serious traction on their priorities in the first 12 to 18 months, they probably never will.

What you should do about it
McKinsey's former managing director Ian Davis and Juniper Networks CEO Kevin Johnson, in separate commentaries, hit on several common themes for successful leadership transitions, such as:

Don't launch a new strategy on day one—but do create a plan for developing one early on.
Devote serious time and energy to deciding how you will allocate your time and energy.
Focus—early—on talent and your top team.
Develop meaningful relationships with members of your board of directors and your chairman.

Letter to a newly appointed CEO

McKinsey's former managing
director Ian Davis offers
advice to a new CEO during his
transition into the role.

McKinsey&Company

London
June 1, 2010

Dear Frank,

It was great to meet for dinner yesterday. Once again, congratulations
on your appointment as CEO. It's a big honour, and an opportunity that I
am sure you will relish.

I am glad that you found our discussion on CEO transitions useful. You
mentioned that it would be helpful to you if I jotted down the key
points we discussed, so I am putting pen to paper. My suggestions are
focused on making a successful leadership transition—not on the
role and attributes of a successful CEO, about which so much has already
been written. They are based primarily on personal observation of
many CEO transitions, as well as on interviews with a number of leading
CEOs and chairmen from around the world.

1. *Context is critical.* As an outside appointment, you must quickly learn about the history, board structure, governance, and national heritage of the company, not to mention its financial performance, morale, and capabilities. Then you must look at this context through the eyes of other constituencies and stakeholders. An early sense of how they might see things is valuable in its own right; it also can help provide a reality check on any assumptions or prejudices, as well as insights, that you may have built up during your interview and recruitment process. Too many CEO transitions get off to a poor start as new leaders learn that what worked in one context doesn't necessarily transfer well to another. Experience is valuable, but it also creates bias. You won't often get such an opportunity or time to step back and reflect, so take it.

2. *We talked about the alleged importance of the first 100 days.* In my view, this is an arbitrary number to be treated with scepticism. In a crisis or turnaround situation, for example, you would not have the luxury of a 100-day transition. In other cases, like the one you are stepping into, you can afford to take a more measured approach. You don't want or need to make decisions on, say, strategy or people or core control processes when you are not confident in your knowledge. There is a big difference between being undecided and indecisive.

   The key is to be thoughtful and purposeful about your transition time frame and to be very clear on what you believe would constitute a successful leadership transition. Set specific transition goals (for example, establishing the trust of your top team and developing a good relationship with your chairman).

   Transitions involve leaving as well as starting. Do not overlook the task of disengaging from your prior job elegantly and professionally. Apart from it being the right thing to do, people will notice and remember. People will also notice and remember how you talk about and acknowledge your predecessor as CEO, and how much respect you have for the past.

3. *Taking over as a new CEO is exhilarating but can also be overwhelming.* A critical task early on is to establish priorities. On day one, you will be handed a list of commitments and meetings. Many of these will be nonnegotiable (for instance, board meetings and annual general meetings), but some will be driven by history and the preferences of your predecessors. Take time to decide which ones you want to attend, bearing in mind the signalling effect your decisions will have.

   Your style in these early transition days and in your first meetings will be watched and noted. It will be important to establish early what you stand for. It will also be important to engage early with employees at all levels to understand the mood and culture and to get a sense of what they actually do and how they feel about the company. People will pay particular attention to how you conduct internal meetings, how you listen, and how much attention you do or do not give to process.

As you establish your priorities, you will need to understand the expectations of the different constituents—for example, your chairman, key investors and analysts, regulators, unions, as well as the people in your organisation. You will receive a lot of advice to set bold expectations, but during the transition period it is more important to *understand* expectations. This understanding will help you stress test your emerging priorities and your degrees of freedom. It will also help you establish your communications approach.

4. *Time will be a big challenge, particularly as your truly discretionary time will be limited.* It will seem that everyone wants a piece of you. This will be true externally and internally. Be ruthless in the use of your time and in what you will and won't do. Avoid developing a habit of cancelling meetings because of time pressures. This will make you look disorganised and will be demoralising to those you stand up. Don't underestimate the possibility and impact of unforeseen events, particularly when things are going well. Leave space for reflection and for crises—you won't know when they will happen, but they will. The rule of thumb is that you can expect at least one potentially career-threatening event a year.

5. *You are fully aware that constructing your top team and building relationships with key people will be a fundamental—perhaps the most important—early task.* In your case, coming in as an external appointment, you will need to get to know the current team and to understand their motivations, capabilities, attitudes to risk, and ways of operating. Be open minded and take time to reassess initial impressions or previous experiences. (This would be all the more true had you been an internal CEO appointment.) As always, don't be shy about biting the bullet if you feel it necessary: it can be easier to make tough calls early in your tenure as CEO. There is always the temptation to surround yourself not just with people you respect but with people with whom you feel comfortable and who are aligned with your way of thinking. This is important, but it can also be important to have a "bit of grit in the oyster." This diversity should enhance the quality of challenge and reduce decision-making bias and risk. It will also send a message of openness to the broader organisation.

6. *Do not underestimate the importance of building a professional, respect-based peer relationship quickly with your board and, particularly, with your chairman.* It's difficult to overstate the importance of the support and confidence of both—you will need them, particularly when the going gets tough. This is a two-way street, of course, but it's essential to invest the necessary time and to start this process early. Do not feel that this is solely the responsibility of the chairman. In particular, observe your chairman closely and get a good feel of how he likes to run the board and how he likes to be kept informed.

    It's useful to remember that the board consists of individuals, each with his or her own experiences, perspectives, and priorities; it's valuable and rewarding to understand these. Remember, it is the board that appointed you and it is the board that is accountable to the company's stakeholders for your success. They, and particularly the chairman, will be as anxious as anyone that you get off to a solid start and establish an effective working relationship with the board, as well as credibility within the organisation.

    As you work on building your relationships with your chairman and board, also make sure that you become familiar with the formal corporate governance principles and company by-laws. Your chairman and key institutional investors will expect it, and you don't want to get caught out on such technicalities.

    There will be many other relationships that could merit your time during the transition period when you are establishing yourself as CEO—for example, with customers, investors, external advisers, media, and suppliers. You will not be able to do them all justice initially, so it's useful to draw up a map of whom you will (and won't) contact and when, based on your judgement of priorities. It may be advisable to share this map with your top team and seek their input. Again, the key thought here is to get control and make mindful choices, rather than letting circumstances or your staff dictate your priorities.

7. *The quality and credibility of your direct-support team will be key.* Your choice of personal assistant and of the support office and technical infrastructure around you will be among your most important (and sometimes most difficult) early decisions. They should both support and reflect your own style and method of operating and be designed to take as much of the burden off your shoulders as

possible. One CEO I know made a big mistake in keeping
his predecessor's assistant and support setup, even though he was
committed to a radical change agenda.

8. *It is advisable to develop—early—a clear transition communications
    strategy, both for internal and external audiences, recognising
    that what appears in the external media has a bigger influence on
    internal and board perceptions than you might initially think.*
    Are you going to be personally visible and accessible to your organisation
    and to your customers, or are you primarily going to delegate
    through the line? How are you going to use communication technol-
    ogies (such as WebEx, blogs, and video messaging) to leverage
    your presence and reach? How will you use management conferences
    to build understanding and alignment? What sort of external
    personal profile do you want or need to have in the media and with
    investors? What role will your chairman play in the company's
    communications and external profile?

    Consistency of message is key. Over time, you will need to develop
    coherent themes and directions that enable you to "tell the story." But
    in the CEO transition period, particularly since you are an outside
    appointment, you may not be clear on your key messages, and, in fact,
    people may not want or expect you to be too specific. In this circum-
    stance, it can be highly effective to focus on your beliefs and what you
    stand for. In time, these can evolve into specific themes that reflect
    your strategic priorities and direction as well as your own style and
    personality. Don't underestimate the damage and confusion that
    can be caused by saying too much too soon or by making promises
    (sometimes unintended) you cannot deliver on subsequently.

9. *A perennial challenge for all in positions of authority is how to get
    objective, balanced feedback and information.* This can be all
    the more problematic in a CEO transition. As soon as an appointment
    is announced, relationships shift in both context and tone. What
    you hear directly will now usually be filtered in some way. People may
    be more prone than usual to tell you what they think you want to
    hear. Conversely, others may overemphasise their criticisms and worries
    in their desire to make an impression or simply to reflect their own
    temperaments and frustrations.

    Successful CEOs use a range of techniques to get around the problem,
    but all involve some form of triangulation and diversity of per-
    spective. The chairman and board have a role to play as do investors,
    customers, and suppliers—it's always advisable to keep an external

orientation to check that the messages from the market are aligned with the messages from within your organisation. Some CEOs use external advisors to help gain perspective; others use more formal techniques such as surveys and systematic feedback mechanisms. Find some room and time for the mavericks inside and outside your organisation. Find some room and time to talk to frontline staff. Most boards review the CEO's performance annually. In your first year, you may well find it helpful to have a six-month review as well. This may sound like unwanted extra pressure, but in reality it will provide additional objective feedback.

You should aim to build your own bulletproof fact base, so challenge data and information that is presented to you, particularly in your early days as CEO. How was it collected? How reliable is it? Have there been any definitional problems in the past? Such a judicious approach will increase your knowledge and confidence in the information you receive (and occasionally, but valuably, they will do the opposite!). They will also send a strong message to your organisation about the importance of accuracy and of making assumptions explicit.

10. *This note is too long already, but one final thought about personal priorities and ground rules.* The CEO role has the structural potential to be all consuming. "The reality is enslavement," a CEO once said to me. It's hard to escape and it's hard to switch off. Nevertheless, there are some tips and techniques that might help. It's important to establish early on how you are prepared to live your CEO life, at least when you are not in those occasional situations that require a 24/7 commitment. Are you going to be routinely available during week-ends for meetings and travel? Will you honour holiday commitments? Do you intend to use air travel as a chance to work or as a chance to relax? Will you routinely go to external functions and dinners? It's important to establish your own pattern and priorities relatively early—not just for you and your family but also to allow your organisation to adjust.

It can be helpful to develop simple habits and rules that reduce stress and wear and tear—examples include not looking at your Blackberry within two hours of going to bed, controlling your accessibility via e-mail or mobile phone, setting limits on alcohol consumption, planning travel meticulously to avoid continental criss-crossing, and setting aside specific time for exercise or nonwork reading. And, as we discussed over dinner, the nine-hour rule has always helped me put sufficient space between my last appointment on one day and my first appointment the following day—and get a reasonable night's sleep.

Finally, don't forget that the role of CEO brings an element of celebrity as well as power, with all the attendant benefits, temptations, and dangers.

●   ●   ●

Frank, I hope this letter is a helpful summary of our discussion. I am attaching a page which summarises the key questions that new CEOs might ask during their transition period. Hopefully it will be a useful checklist for you over the next months. As I have said, there are few absolute rights and wrongs, but it is important to make mindful choices about each of them. I will obviously be interested to hear of your experiences and feedback.

In the meantime, as we discussed, I will set up meetings with a few other CEOs. I'm sure you will enjoy getting to know them and that they will form a useful peer group and sounding board for you.

Best of luck in what I am sure will be a great experience. I look forward to catching up with you in a month or so—my turn to pay this time.

Yours ever,

CEO transition checklist

1. *Have I reflected on the context of my transition—not just from my own perspective, but from that of all key stakeholders?*

2. *Have I established, in my own mind, the time frame and intended outcomes of my leadership transition?*

3. *Have I established my initial set of priorities with a full understanding of what others expect of me?*

4. *How will I control my agenda and allocate my time?*

5. *Have I developed a clear process and time frame for selecting my top team?*

6. *Have I committed sufficiently to building a relationship with my chairman and board?*

7. *Do I have a mechanism for building the necessary support office and infrastructure?*

8. *Have I thought through my communications plan—internal and external?*

9. *Do I have a mechanism for getting balanced feedback and information?*

10. *Have I established appropriate personal ground rules?*

My transition story

The head of Juniper Networks
discusses his strategy
for making the transition into
the CEO role.

When Kevin Johnson took the reins at Juniper
Networks, in September 2008, he left a role
that was, by some measures, much bigger: in his
previous position, as president of Microsoft's
platform and services division, he had been responsible for more than $20 billion in revenue, including
the company's lucrative Windows business.
By contrast, the sales at Juniper, a provider of IT
networking infrastructure, were $3.3 billion
during Johnson's first full year as CEO.

The timing of his start date didn't make his transition
easy. During Johnson's first week, Lehman
Brothers collapsed and the global macroeconomic
landscape changed dramatically. This required
some quick moves: a doubling down on big R&D
bets, for example, combined with significant
cuts in other operating costs. All the while, Johnson
tried to follow a set of transition principles that

he described recently in an interview with McKinsey's Endre Holen and Allen Webb.

Johnson's suggestions: Seek advice before day one on the job. Don't come in with a new strategy; instead, use your first few months to connect with the organization, set the strategic agenda, and shape a talent plan. Bring your top managers and your board along with you. Be very deliberate about how you will effect needed cultural changes. And don't underestimate the increased scope of your new role.

Learning before starting

My appointment as Juniper's CEO was announced in late July 2008, and I went to work in early September. During those six weeks, I was wrapping up my responsibilities at Microsoft, but I also spent time with five different CEOs, asking them for their advice on the job and the transition. Each of them gave me an interesting perspective from a slightly different angle.

One message was the need to be thoughtful about how your direct reports and the executive staff would see the transition. Juniper's previous CEO, Scott Kriens, had been in that job for 12 or so years, almost since the time the company was started. A lot of people had invested their careers in Juniper and wondered whether I was going to clean house. So one of the CEOs I talked with told me that it's important to assess the talent quickly and then be clear with them—either you're going to keep them or you're not—but you shouldn't leave it vague, which isn't helpful either for them or for you.

Another point was the importance of having the former CEO there to help you when you need his or her ideas and input, but not making him or her extremely visible for the whole organization, because it's hard for people to disconnect from the previous leader and establish a connection to the new one. A CEO I spoke with had recently succeeded a long-tenured CEO. That discussion helped me understand that the previous

leader—especially one who's still on the board or has some other role—
may be going through an emotional disconnect from the organization,
while you're trying to engage with it. You have to be sensitive to that
reality and figure out how you can make the best use of the previous CEO's
expertise, knowledge, and talent, but also how you can get enough room
to establish your own leadership agenda and connection with the team.

In my situation, Scott Kriens was phenomenal: he gave me the breathing
room to establish my leadership agenda—which I'm sure was hard for
him because he had put so much energy into his work—but he was there
for me as well. For the first few months, Scott and I found that having
dinner every other week gave us two or three hours when I could share my
observations and thinking with him and get his thoughts too.

The first few months

I was hired to scale up the company and take it to the next level. The
status quo wasn't going to get us there, and I didn't have all the time in
the world. One CEO I talked with emphasized that when you come
in, you've got a certain period of time to put an agenda on the table, and if
you haven't made enough of the changes you need to make in the first
12 to 18 months, it's going to be too late.

My personal opinion is that from day one, you should have a point of view
about the business: "Hey, this is a good company; this is a good industry,"
or "This a good industry, but our company's in trouble." That doesn't mean
that you translate your point of view into a new strategy on day one.
But by the end of your first couple of months, you'd better have a basic idea
of your long-term goals, the strategy to get there, and what you've
got to do about leadership and talent over the next 12 months or so.

Before even starting on the job, I put together a plan of what I wanted
to accomplish in the first 100 days: how I would invest my time and the
key people I needed to connect with—the leadership team, employees,
key customers, investors, partners, and the board. When I showed up on
the first day, I used this plan to communicate with the team about
how I would approach the transition. In the first week, I connected with
my direct reports, sent an e-mail to all employees, and set up my
calendar. But five days after I started, Lehman Brothers declared bankruptcy
and the global economy changed dramatically. I continued to work
on the 100-day plan, but in parallel I was trying to digest everything that
was happening in the economy. That was probably a very unusual
transition, but I'd expect all of them to have some serious issue—internal
or external—that wasn't anticipated.

My objective for the 100-day plan was primarily to connect with different constituents, listen and learn, start testing some ideas, and begin to shape the strategic agenda. In week one, I asked my direct reports to sit down together as a group and answer four questions: what are you most proud of about Juniper and why, what needs to change and why, what do you hope I do as the new CEO, and what are you most afraid I might do as the new CEO? Those four questions gave me a very quick read on the situation, opened up an interesting dialogue with my direct reports, and helped me to feel comfortable.

After I asked the questions, I left the room for an hour or so to let my direct reports work through their answers collectively. I wanted them to talk as a group without me because that would allow them to be candid and anonymous. They wrote down the answers on a whiteboard anonymously, so I didn't know whose individual point of view each answer reflected. I also had the HR executive summarize the answers, which I then discussed with the team.

Then over the first three months, I took the top 100 or so people in the company and had a one-hour one-on-one session with each of them. I also did two-hour business reviews with every business group. And at the end of my first 100 days, I wrote a memo. It didn't state specific solutions or actions but instead focused on my early observations about the company's business, strategy, people, culture, and competition— issues that we ought to be thinking about. I shared the memo with the top 100 people in the company. The memo forced me to digest everything I had learned and allowed me to communicate my thoughts in a consistent way with each person who got it. People could think, "OK, Kevin did all of these one-on-ones, and at least I get to see what he took away from them," instead of, "Oh, wow, he spent all of this time doing these one-on-ones; I wonder if he learned anything?"

Four months after I started at Juniper, I had each of my direct reports conduct a people review with me on their organizations, their talent, and an assessment of their direct reports. That allowed me to learn what my direct reports thought about their people and where we had gaps. This review was the basis for a board meeting where I took our directors through an all-up assessment of Juniper's talent. Three months later, I took the leadership team through a strategy review process in a very structured way, and that fed the next board meeting. These management exercises allowed me to take the organization and the board along on a quest for the right answers—our long-term goals and the strategy that would help us achieve them.

Particularly in the beginning, it's important to look at the way you sequence decisions and actions. For the compensation model, especially, there was a very specific window of opportunity. Since I started in September and our fiscal year begins in January, I knew that if I didn't do that by January 1, it would take me another year. So I did it within the first 100 days, which allowed me to communicate what I thought was important and how our rewards systems should reflect this.

By the end of the first few months, I had spent time listening and learning, developing our long-term goals and strategy, and made some important decisions on people and reward systems. This was the beginning of my journey.

Shaping the culture

As I've said, Lehman Brothers and the economy tanked five days after I took over at Juniper. I actually found the crisis somewhat helpful, because whenever you have a compelling event—an economic crisis, a competitive attack, a huge product launch—it brings teams together. It puts you in the battlefield immediately, and teams bond and get to know one another on the battlefield; that's where relationships are created, tested, and strengthened. Besides bringing our team closer together, the economic collapse gave people a compelling reason to accept change. They now had a different mind-set: this is no longer business as usual.

Often you have to change not only the people and strategy but also the culture. For example, when I asked people what they were most proud of at Juniper they would say, "Our culture of collaboration and innovation." When I asked them what they hoped I would change, often they would say, "We avoid conflict as a culture and try to get to consensus on everything, so sometimes we're paralyzed in making hard decisions." Embracing what's great about a culture and at the same time injecting new elements into it can be challenging.

To tackle cultural issues, I put together a team of about 40 employees. Some had been with the company for 1 or 2 years, some for 12 or 14 years. They came from every discipline—sales, R&D, finance, HR. We got support from a consultant, Ann Rhoades, who had been chief people officer at Southwest Airlines and Jet Blue. Ann and her team organized a two-day work session with the Juniper team, where we talked about the company's culture. I was able to listen, share ideas, and help influence the result, but the output of this session primarily came from these 40 people, who really understood the values that make us what we are. I took those values to the company's top 30 executives and we massaged them again. Eventually, we ended up with five.[1]

[1] Juniper's five values appear online at juniper.net/us/en/company/profile/value.

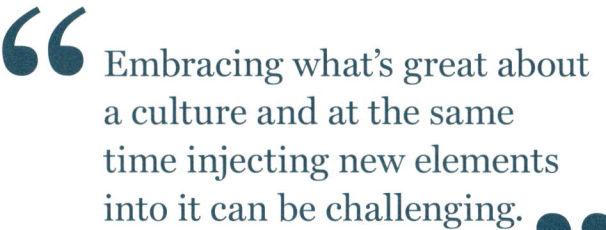

> Embracing what's great about a culture and at the same time injecting new elements into it can be challenging.

Kevin Johnson is the CEO of Juniper Networks. Prior to joining Juniper, he spent 16 years with Microsoft Corporation, including serving as president of the platforms and services division and group vice president of the worldwide sales, marketing, and services organization.

This process allowed me to embrace the great things about the culture of the past and amplify them, and then inject the new things we needed for our future. And those values have been translated into behaviors. For example, we now say, "Here are the behaviors that would demonstrate a given value for someone in a sales role." The values are woven into the performance reviews too and into the way we recognize outstanding employees. The company never really celebrated successes as much as we needed to, so we launched an awards program. Every quarter, I give out three CEO awards. Each winner gets up to $100,000 of equity and public recognition. We use rewards to recognize people we want others to see as role models.

Adapting to the scope of the CEO role

I came to Juniper from running a really big organization at Microsoft. You might think that the new job was simpler, but that would confuse scope with scale. Some of the big-scale jobs I had at Microsoft—running worldwide sales, marketing, and services, for example—had a defined scope: basically, running field operations. One thing I noticed in running things at scale is that once you get to a certain point, the numbers are bigger but the challenges and responsibilities aren't. Running $20 billion in revenue isn't much different, by itself, from running $30 billion. The numbers are bigger, but the things that you do and the skills you need to lead a growing organization are basically the same. By contrast, expanding into different customer segments, adding new core businesses, and taking on a broader range of initiatives all increase the scope, complexity, and challenge of a job.

When I came to Juniper, all of the things that I learned at Microsoft about scaling up an organization were very applicable. But my new role at Juniper also expanded the scope of my responsibilities to new areas, including investor relations, managing a board, and allocating resources across a company. Now I had responsibility for an end-to-end business with multiple business groups and a wide range of products, services, and customer segments. I have to create the conditions so that these groups can innovate and create new products and technologies, to create the right environment for sales and marketing, to get enough time for investor relations, to engage with the board, to understand my role under Sarbanes–Oxley, to close big deals. The scope of the job is much wider.

This kind of expanded scope opens up new experiences. One new thing for me as CEO was communicating with the financial community. And I made some mistakes here. When the economic downturn hit, we decided that, strategically, continuing to fund R&D and customer satisfaction were the two most important things for the company. When so many others were laying off huge numbers of workers, we increased investment in R&D and customer satisfaction. Meanwhile, we cut operational expenditures in every other part of the business.

On my first earnings call, I stressed the importance of investments in R&D and customer satisfaction. I was less clear about reducing our overall operational expenses. All the analysts heard was the increase in investment. At a time when some people were saying, "Kevin, you should lay off 10 to 15 percent of your workforce today," I was saying that we were going to increase investment in R&D. The analysts thought I was a coconut head. I had to communicate more clearly and completely so that people could understand how we would operate during the downturn. We did reduce overall operating expenses while still managing to increase our investment in R&D. We even exceeded our expectations on operating margins. I think that we earned a lot of credibility; it always has to be earned.

Dealing with a board as CEO was also a new experience. I had been involved with boards before, but as CEO I'm accountable to them in a new way. I faced the question of how often to communicate with our board and in what way—one-on-one or collectively? It's important to stay connected with board members and to give them a perspective between board meetings. I use a combination of approaches. Sometimes I'll call individual directors on certain topics and discuss them one-on-one. Other times I may ask the whole board to meet with the leadership team on a specific topic.

I also found that it's very helpful to send periodic e-mails to directors on strategic topics and events. If there are significant things I want our directors to know about, I shoot them a quick e-mail: here's an update on three topics—boom, boom, boom. When we get to the next board meeting, these e-mails have kept everyone up to date on important topics, and we don't have to bring everyone up to speed on everything. This was very important in my first few months because it gave the board more opportunities to understand how I approach issues and engage with people than they would get from board meetings alone. o

Endre Holen is a director in McKinsey's Seattle office, where Allen Webb is a member of McKinsey Publishing. Copyright © 2010 McKinsey & Company. All rights reserved. We welcome your comments on this article. Please send them to quarterly_comments@mckinsey.com.

Why good bosses tune in to their people

Robert I. Sutton

Stanford management professor Bob Sutton offers some pointed advice for those at the top of organizations. Know how to project power, he counsels, since those you lead need to believe you have it for it to be effective. And to lock in your team's loyalty, boldly defend their backs.

The problem

As the boss, you are the most important person in the organization, and subordinates monitor, magnify, and mimic your every move. You need to stay in tune with this relentless attention and use it to your advantage.

Why it matters

Your success and influence as boss depends on correctly reading those with whom you interact most frequently and intensely. Because your leadership style reverberates throughout the organization, ultimately it will bolster or undermine company performance and culture.

What you should do about it

The first and most important task is to convince others that you are in charge, otherwise your job will be impossible and your tenure short. Second, boost your subordinates' performance by "watching their backs": making it possible for them to learn, take intelligent risks, and feel pride and dignity along the way.

Bosses matter. They matter because more than 95 percent of all people in the workforce have bosses, are bosses, or both. They matter because they set the tone for their followers and organizations. And they matter because many studies show that for more than 75 percent of employees, dealing with their immediate boss is the most stressful part of the job. Lousy bosses can kill you—literally. A 2009 Swedish study tracking 3,122 men for ten years found that those with bad bosses suffered 20 to 40 percent more heart attacks than those with good bosses.

Bosses matter to everyone they oversee, but they matter most to those just beneath them in the pecking order: the people they guide at close range, who constantly tangle with the boss's virtues, foibles, and quirks. Whether you are the CEO of a Fortune 500 company or the head chef at a restaurant, your success depends on staying in tune with the people you interact with most frequently and intensely.

All bosses matter, but those at the top matter most. Whether or not they know it, their followers monitor, magnify, and often mimic their moves. I worked with a large company where the CEO did almost all of the talking in meetings, interrupted everyone, and silenced dissenting underlings. His executive vice presidents complained about him behind his back, but when he left the room, the most powerful EVP started acting the very same way. When that EVP left, the next-highest-ranking boss began imitating him in turn.

Robert Sutton is a professor of management science and engineering at Stanford University. This article is adapted from his forthcoming book, *Good Boss, Bad Boss: How to Be the Best . . . and Learn from the Worst,* to be published by Business Plus in September 2010.

The ripple effects of this CEO's style are consistent with findings from peer-reviewed studies showing that senior executives' actions can reverberate throughout organizations, ultimately undermining or bolstering their cultures and performance levels. When CEOs have far more pay and power than their direct reports do, for instance, performance can suffer if their subordinates feel they can't stop them from making and implementing lousy decisions. A few years ago, I did a workshop with a management team struggling with "group dynamics" problems. Team members felt that their boss, a senior vice president, listened poorly and "ran over" others; he called his people "thin-skinned wimps." I asked the team—the senior vice president and five direct reports—to do an exercise. The six of them spent 20 minutes brainstorming potential products and then narrowed their choices to the most feasible, the wildest, and the most likely to fail.

As they brainstormed, I counted the number of comments made by each team member and the number of times each interrupted someone else and was interrupted in turn. The senior vice president contributed about 65 percent of the comments, interrupted others at least 20 times, and was never interrupted. When I had him leave the room, I asked his subordinates to estimate the results, and they did so accurately. Then the senior vice president returned. He recalled making about 25 percent of the comments, interrupting others perhaps 3 times, and being interrupted 3 or 4 times. When I showed him the results and explained that his direct reports had estimated them far more accurately, he was flabbergasted and annoyed.

Being a boss, as this exercise shows, often resembles the role of a high-status primate: your subordinates watch you constantly, so they know more about you than you know about them. Likewise, anthropologists who study chimpanzees, gorillas, and baboons report that followers devote far more attention to their leader than he devotes to them. (Studies of baboon troops show that typical members glance at the dominant male every 20 or 30 seconds.) As Princeton University psychologist Susan Fiske observes, primates—including ourselves—"pay attention to those who control their outcomes."

Linda Hudson, CEO of BAE Systems, got this message after becoming the first female president of General Dynamics. After her first day on the job, a dozen women in her office imitated how she tied her scarf. Hudson realized, "It really was now about me and the context of setting the tone for the organization. That was a lesson I have never forgotten—that as a leader, people are looking at you in a way that you could not have imagined in other roles." Hudson added that such scrutiny and the consequent responsibility is "something that I think about virtually every day."

The best bosses work doggedly to stay in tune with this relentless attention and use it to their advantage. They are self-absorbed, but not for selfish reasons. On the contrary, they know that the success of their people and organizations depends on maintaining an accurate view of how others construe their moods and moves—and responding with rapid, effective adjustments.

That view is invaluable for bosses as they try to carry out their first and most important task: convincing others that they are in charge. Bosses who fail to do this will find their jobs impossible, their lives hell, and their tenures short. Of course, taking charge effectively isn't enough. The best bosses also boost performance by watching their people's backs:

making it safe for them to learn, act, and take intelligent risks; shielding them from unnecessary distractions and external idiocy of every stripe; and doing hundreds more little things that help them achieve one small win after another—and feel pride and dignity along the way.

Taking control

James Meindl's research on "the romance of leadership"[1] shows that leaders get far more credit—and blame—than they deserve, largely because, cognitively, it is easier and more emotionally satisfying to treat leadership as the primary cause of performance than to consider the convoluted and often subtle mishmash of factors that actually determine performance differences. It is especially difficult to resist demonizing the bosses of failing organizations, however irrational that may be. This bias toward glorifying and vilifying individual leaders (and downplaying the role of systems, collective action, and external factors outside management's influence) is especially strong in the United States and many European nations.

Yet the best evidence shows that bosses rarely account for more than 15 percent of the gap between good and bad organizational performance—although they often get more than 50 percent of the credit and blame. If you are a boss, this is your lot in life; make the best of it. If you claim that you don't have much influence over what happens to the team or company you lead, your people will lose confidence in you and your superiors will send you packing. Here are four suggestions for magnifying the illusion of control (for more ideas, see the checklist, "Tricks for taking charge," on page 140):

1. Express confidence even if you don't feel it

In 2002, I heard Andy Grove, Intel's legendary CEO (1987–98), interviewed by Harvard University's Clay Christensen, who asked Andy how leaders can act and feel confident despite their doubts. He answered, "Investment decisions or personnel decisions and prioritization don't wait for that picture to be clarified. You have to make them when you have to make them." That's why executives need to use what I call the faking-it-until-you-make-it strategy, which he also touched on: "Part of it is self-discipline, and part of it is deception. And the deception becomes reality. It is deception in the sense that you pump yourself up and put a better face on things than you start off feeling. But after a while, if you act confident, you become more confident."[2]

[1] James R. Meindl and Sanford B. Ehrlich, "The romance of leadership and the evaluation of organizational performance," *Academy of Management*, 1987, Volume 30, Number 1, pp. 91–109.
[2] Clayton Christensen interviewed Andrew Grove at a Harvard Business School Conference in Cupertino, California, on October 3, 2002. I attended this session, and the organizers provided me a transcript, which is the source for these quotations from Andy Grove.

Research showing that "belief follows behavior" supports his argument. And confidence is especially crucial for inspiring your followers, because like all emotions, it's contagious—especially when displayed by closely scrutinized bosses.

2. Don't dither

Indecision, delay, and waffling are the hallmarks of a crummy boss; the best ones know that crisp and seemingly quick decisions bolster the illusion (and reality) that they are in charge. As late stage director Frank Hauser said, "You have three weapons: 'Yes,' 'No,' and 'I don't know.' Use them. Don't dither; you can always change your mind later. Nobody minds that. What they do mind is the two minutes of agonizing when all the actor has asked is, 'Do I get up now?'"

3. Get and give credit

A great thing about being the boss is that when your people do good work, you usually get too much of the credit. Smart bosses often use this to their advantage, knowing that people want to work for and do business with winners.

As a boss, you may already use subtle tactics to get credit, such as collaborating with people who are likely to praise you (so that you don't have to brag) and, when you do mention your accomplishments, giving copious credit to others. David Kelley, the modest chairman and founder of design firm IDEO, is a master of the art of giving his people credit. I believe that one reason IDEO became a renowned innovation firm under David's leadership is that he relentlessly thanks others for making him look good, gives them credit when the company does something great, and downplays his contribution—something I have observed him do hundreds of times over the past 15 years.

Indeed, the best bosses routinely give their followers more credit than they probably deserve. And when bosses do this, everyone wins. As the boss, you will get the lion's share of credit because of the romance of leadership. Your immediate team will regard you as truthful. And your modesty and generosity will be admired—especially by outsiders, who will see you as both competent and generous.

4. Blame yourself

In August 2008, I listened on the radio as Maple Leaf Foods CEO Michael McCain made a statement about the deaths and illnesses traced to tainted meats produced by one of his company's plants. McCain's voice quivered as he announced its closure, apologized to the victims, and said that the people at Maple Leaf—including himself—were responsible and that it was his job to restore faith in the company.

His response is striking because it is so rare yet so consistent with research on how to fuel the illusion (and reality) that the boss is in charge. Unlike many people in such a predicament, McCain accepted the fact that he would be held responsible for what his people did, no matter what. When something important happens, the boss is expected to know. Rather than blaming others, McCain understood it was wiser to accept the blame and learn from it. Leaders who denounce outside forces for their troubles come across as disingenuous and powerless. By refusing to take responsibility, they implicitly raise a damning question: "If you didn't have the power to break it, how can you have the power to fix it?" The public also sees a boss's refusal to accept responsibility as a sign that nothing has been learned from the errors.

Bosses who ignore and stomp on their subordinates' humanity sometimes generate quick gains. But in the long run, such shortsightedness undermines creativity, efficiency, and commitment.

If you as a boss want to enhance the perception that you are in charge—and fuel performance at the same time—taking at least some of the blame is usually necessary. Experiments by University of Michigan professor Fiona Lee and her colleagues show that managers who take responsibility for problems like pay freezes and failed projects are seen as more powerful, competent, and likeable than those who deny responsibility. In another study, Lee's group examined stock price fluctuations in 14 companies over 21 years. They found that when top executives accepted responsibility for problems, stock prices were consistently higher afterward than when CEOs denied responsibility.

The key, though, is not just to accept blame and apologize. You must also take immediate control in whatever way you can, show that you and your people have learned from failure, announce new plans, and, when they are implemented, make sure everyone understands that things are improving because of them—just as Michael McCain did. Although no one can predict his company's ultimate fate, the Canadian press praised McCain for his clarity, compassion, and control. A nationwide survey in December 2008 showed that among Canadians, confidence in the Maple Leaf brand had risen to 91 percent, from 60 percent, since August of that year. Although the company reported losses in 2008, it returned to profitability in 2009. As McCain said in February 2010, "The packaged-meats business continues to recover. Our brands and our reputation are intact"[3]—an assessment most analysts and customers echoed.

Bolstering performance

Bosses who ignore and stomp on their subordinates' humanity sometimes generate quick gains. But in the long run, such short-sightedness usually undermines their followers' creativity, efficiency, and commitment. The best bosses focus on boosting the performance of their people through stratagems such as the three that follow:

1. Provide psychological safety

Good bosses spark imagination and encourage learning by creating a safety zone where people can talk about half-baked ideas, test them, and even make big mistakes without fear of ridicule, punishment, or ostracism. I witnessed the power of psychological safety at a large media company where a new CEO was determined to drive out fear. A vice president had launched a magazine that ended up being an expensive, well-publicized flop. She would have been demoted and fired—and probably publicly humiliated—under past regimes. Instead, the CEO spoke at a gathering and congratulated her for her courage and skill. He emphasized that the decision to start the magazine wasn't just hers; senior management had backed it. After his speech, every executive I spoke with portrayed the CEO's comments as a watershed event.

An absence of psychological safety, in concert with fear of the boss, can be dangerous or downright deadly. Studies by Harvard Business School professor Amy Edmondson and her colleagues show that when nurses fear their supervisors will punish and humiliate them for making mistakes, they hesitate to report their drug-treatment errors. The hazards of fearing authority also emerge from research with commercial pilots in flight simulators. One study showed that when pilots faked mild incapacitation toward the end of a rough and rainy simulated flight, their copilots failed to take the controls 25 percent of the time— resulting in simulated crashes. The copilots knew the pilots were incapacitated yet failed to question their authority. Dysfunctional

[3] John Spears, "Maple Leaf Foods returns to profit," *Toronto Star*, February 25, 2010.

deference can kill real flight crews and passengers too. In 1979, a commuter plane crashed, in part, because the second officer failed to take control when the captain, a vice president known for gruffness, became partly incapacitated.

2. Shield people

The best bosses invent, borrow, and implement ways to reduce the mental and emotional load heaped on their followers—and protect them from the incompetence, cluelessness, and premature judgments of fellow bosses or others who can undermine their followers' work and well being. Followers who enjoy such protection (and who may be bosses themselves) have the freedom to take risks and try new things.

Annette Kyle, for example, managed some 60 employees at a Texas terminal where they loaded chemicals from railcars onto ships and trucks. In the mid-1990s, Annette led a "revolution" that dramatically raised her unit's performance through a host of changes, including better planning, greater responsibility at the lowest levels, improved and more transparent metrics, and numerous cultural changes. She personally sewed "no whining" patches on workers' uniforms, for example, to discourage the local penchant for complaining and auctioned off her desk to workers for $60 because, as she explained it, "I shouldn't be sitting behind a big desk. I should be contributing to team goals however possible."

This transformation virtually eliminated the penalties that were levied when ships arrived at the terminal's dock but (despite considerable advance warning) workers weren't ready to load them. These "demurrage charges," which cost the company $2.5 million the year before the revolution, were down to $10,000 the year after. Previously, it had taken more than three hours to load an average truck. Afterward, more than 90 percent were loaded within an hour of arrival. Surveys and interviews by University of Southern California researchers showed that employees became more satisfied with their jobs and felt proud of their accomplishments. I asked Annette how she could make such radical changes in her giant company. She answered that her boss shielded her from top-ranking managers—he found the resources and experts she needed but never discussed these moves with senior management until they succeeded.

Good bosses are especially adept at protecting their people's time—for example, by eliminating needless meetings. Take a cue from Will Wright, designer of computer games such as *The Sims*: rather than automatically scheduling meetings, ask yourself if they are really needed. Wright employed a clever trick. Every time someone called a meeting, he charged that person a dollar. Although he collected a lot of dollars, this requirement made people "think twice, even though it was only a dollar." He also used an employee-centered method to keep meetings short—

inviting the creative but impatient artist Ocean Quigley, "the canary in the coal mine." When Quigley raised his hand to be excused, "we knew that the meeting had hit diminishing returns."

3. Make small gestures

The late Robert Townsend, CEO of Avis and author of the masterpiece *Up the Organization,* called the phrase "thank you" a "really neglected form of compensation." The broader lesson for bosses is the importance of "the attitude of gratitude," a line borrowed from Kimberly Wiefling, founder of Wiefling Consulting, who argues that too many projects end without acknowledgement and celebration and that whether a project succeeds or fails, the best managers take time to express appreciation. Conveying this attitude is especially crucial when the stench of failure fills the air—precisely the time when people most need support from the boss and one another. Bosses with the will and the skill to provide that kind of support set the stage for learning from fiascos. Unfortunately, too many bosses have the opposite response and use such occasions to conduct "blamestorms" or "circular fire squads," where the goal is to point fingers, humiliate the guilty, and throw a few overboard.

●   ●   ●

Good bosses don't just get more from their people and do it in more civilized ways; they attract and keep better people. If you think your employees are deadbeats, downers, and jerks, look in the mirror. Why don't the best people want to work for you? Why do people who appeared to be stars when they joined your team seem to turn rotten?

Of all the skills and aspirations good bosses must have, self-awareness is probably the most important. Cornell University's David Dunning has shown that poor performers consistently overestimate their intellectual and social skills. In contrast, the best performers accurately judge both their strengths and their flaws. Dunning's research has crucial implications for leadership. The best and worst bosses alike suffer from overconfidence and insecurity, from weaknesses and blind spots. Such is the human condition. Yet the best bosses are keenly aware of their flaws, work to overcome them and to reverse the resulting damage, and enlist others who can compensate for their weaknesses.

The most effective bosses devote enormous effort to understanding how their moods, quirks, skills, and actions affect their followers' performance and humanity. They constantly make adjustments to be a bit more helpful and constructive tomorrow than they were yesterday. To be a great boss, you must constantly ask and try to answer many questions. Perhaps the most crucial is, "What does it feel like to work for me?" If your people answered this question honestly, would they say that you know the impact your words and deeds have on them—or that you are living in a fool's paradise? ○

Using rivalry to spur innovation

The problem
Modern companies have embraced many of the elements that made the Italian Renaissance such an innovative period. But some still overlook the ability of productive rivalry to stimulate innovation.

Why it matters
According to Mark Little, the director of General Electric's Global Research Group, the use of productive rivalry has made a difference in his company's efforts to develop better aircraft engines, composite materials, and power generation equipment.

What you should do about it
If your R&D group doesn't employ rivalry, look for opportunities to form teams, appreciate differences in their respective approaches, and conduct market tests. Embedding rivalry in a culture where what's celebrated most is the outcome— a better product or service— can be a powerful positive force.

The art of innovation

Bernard T. Ferrari and Jessica Goethals

Companies looking for new sources of creative energy might want to look backward— to the productive rivalry that catalyzed much of the artistic innovation during the Italian Renaissance.

Business leaders tend to raise their eyebrows when they read about parallels between history and modern management—and for good reason. There are undoubtedly many people who offer better leadership lessons than Attila the Hun, and it is unclear whether Alexander the Great can tell us much about business strategy. So it's with some trepidation that we set forth the premise of this article: that the Italian Renaissance was such an extraordinary period of creativity it can shed light on how to stimulate business innovation.

We're quite conscious of other great eras of innovation—the 18th-century industrial revolution in Great Britain, the late-19th-century emergence of managerial capitalism in the United States, and even the present period of digital innovation. One thing that's striking about the Renaissance, though, is that it took place on a scale not very different from that of many large, modern enterprises. Northern Italy is no larger than the state of Michigan, and at the beginning of the 15th century, the three great centers of Renaissance creativity—Florence, Rome, and Venice—had a combined population of roughly 200,000.[1]

Bernie Ferrari is an alumnus of McKinsey's Los Angeles and New York offices, where he was a director; he is currently the chairman of Ferrari Consultancy. Jessica Goethals is a PhD candidate in Italian Studies at New York University.

[1] See Elizabeth S. Cohen and Thomas V. Cohen, *Daily Life in Renaissance Italy*, Westport, CT: Greenwood Publishing Group, 2001, p. 7; Peter Partner, *Renaissance Rome 1500–1559: A Portrait of a Society*, Berkeley, CA: University of California Press, 1980, p. 82; and Richard A. Goldthwaite, *The Building of Renaissance Florence: An Economic and Social History*, Baltimore, MD: Johns Hopkins University Press, 1982, p. 33.

The ability of a population and region of this size to generate creative output—ranging from the world's largest masonry dome to linear perspective, modern-day portrait painting, technical breakthroughs in glassblowing and bronze casting, the italic type of the Aldine Press, sfumato and chiaroscuro, and the designs in Leonardo's sketchbooks— makes it, in our opinion, intriguing for innovation-minded leaders. What's more, there are some uncanny parallels between what went on during the Renaissance and principles that have proven their worth in R&D organizations—such as collision between diverse experts, providing loose guidelines, and establishing stretch goals.

Less in line with mainstream R&D practices: the degree to which Renaissance creativity was built on professional rivalries—like the ones between Leonardo, Michelangelo, Raphael, and Titian—that are commonly viewed as some of the most productive in history. It may be that by overlooking the potential of rivalry, modern R&D organizations are missing an opportunity to promote ground-breaking innovation.

What we've already learned from the Renaissance

Some of the practices that made the Renaissance such a creative period have already been largely integrated into today's R&D labs.

Promoting 'collision'

Consider, for example, the popular notion that constant collision between engineers, scientists, and managers will lead to better collaboration and ultimately yield the best ideas. The classic manifestation of collision is the multidisciplinary corporate R&D lab, where innovators of different stripes are gathered together in a single research facility. Among the most famous of these facilities are IBM's Watson Research Center, HP Labs, Bell Labs, and GE's Global Research Center. Virtual spaces, if built correctly, can also be effective for encouraging collision. Take the example of Tata's Innoverse hub. This portal serves as a virtual innovation forum where employees from across Tata's business units can post ideas, comment on them, and then vote on the ones they like the best. In one year, it gathered 12,000 ideas, on topics ranging from R&D to management and strategy, several hundred of which have been turned into projects or implemented through operational reforms.[2]

The concept of collision resonates with the creative energy of the Renaissance. Italy at the time was one of the most urban regions of Europe, and its cities, although small by modern standards, were densely packed centers teeming with painters, craftsmen, and sculptors.[3] Rome, for example, attracted throughout Italy flocks of artists who were seeking

[2] Jessie Scanlon, "How to build a culture of innovation," *BusinessWeek*, August 19, 2009.
[3] See Elizabeth S. Cohen and Thomas V. Cohen, *Daily Life in Renaissance Italy*, Westport, CT: Greenwood Publishing Group, 2001, pp. 7–8.

the patronage of the Vatican. The relatively small urban space forced them into frequent and often intense interactions with one another. Artists benefited from the diversity of the colleagues around them, and the high rates of collision with these peers allowed them to learn from one another, exchange ideas and techniques, and build off one another's diverse accomplishments.

Giving researchers their space

Many of the world's greatest inventions have been stumbled on by mistake. Smart R&D managers recognize this and allow their researchers to turn mistaken or unexpected findings into new lines of research, products, or technologies. Recently, there has been much discussion of Google's policy that allows researchers to spend time on their own ideas, projects, or personal development. It's not a new idea. 3M has long allowed its employees to spend 15 percent of their time on projects of their own choosing.[4] Similarly, at Tata Consultancy Services, each employee receives 5 hours of a 45-hour work week for personal projects.[5]

The Renaissance equivalent of setting R&D guidelines was the commission—say, for a painting or piece of architecture. These contracts would stipulate a subject to be painted, who would paint which parts of the work, the dimensions and medium of the painting, the timeline, and the amount of money to be paid. Although at times these contracts could be quite specific, during the Renaissance, artists' prominence in society grew, so that they increasingly could negotiate contracts that allowed for creative interpretation and stylistic flexibility.

Michelangelo's painting of the Sistine Chapel's ceiling is a fine example of how an artist's higher social position translated into greater negotiating leverage with patrons. In 1506, Pope Julius II decided to complete the painting of the interior of the chapel (the walls had been painted 20 years earlier) with a grandiose fresco across the entire ceiling. He went to Michelangelo, who was well known as a sculptor (though not much as a painter), and asked him to take on the job. Only after some cajoling did Michelangelo agree. In the initial contract, the Pope proposed a scheme of 12 enormous figures of the Apostles. Michelangelo convinced the Pope to agree to a much grander subject that documented humanity's need for salvation. Michelangelo later bragged that he had gotten the Pope to allow him "to do as I liked."[6] The artist's ability to negotiate for flexibility contributed to the remarkable creation that is the Sistine Chapel ceiling.

Setting stretch goals

Smart companies establish practices and programs that encourage innovators to "shoot for the stars." Consider, for example, Royal Dutch/

[4] Jessie Scanlon, "How 3M encourages collaboration," *BusinessWeek*, September 2, 2009.
[5] Jessie Scanlon, "How to build a culture of innovation," *BusinessWeek*, August 19, 2009.
[6] Loren Partridge, *The Art of Renaissance Rome 1400–1600*, New York: Prentice Hall, 1996, p. 17.

Smart companies establish practices and programs that encourage innovators to "shoot for the stars."

Shell's GameChanger program, which is designed to seek out and finance good ideas that have a low chance of coming to fruition but could have a profoundly positive effect on Shell's business. GameChanger teams in each of Shell's business units vet, select, and then support ideas as they are developed. Ideas can come from within the company or from outside innovators, although Shell retains the intellectual-property rights to any designs or products that might be generated. The company devotes 10 percent of its innovation budget to the program, which generates fully 30 percent of Shell's R&D projects. By recognizing the power of good but far-fetched ideas, Shell has reaped the benefits of a number of new technologies that few thought were possible to achieve.

Similarly, the masters of the Renaissance were constantly setting for themselves artistic and engineering goals that were beyond reasonable reach. When Brunelleschi arrived in Rome, he set to work studying the remarkable architectural masterpiece that is the Roman Pantheon. The structure's dome, in particular, fascinated him: he was awestruck by the sheer amount of space that it covered and puzzled over how such a feat of engineering had been achieved. Then the city of Florence began construction of its now-famous Basilica di Santa Maria del Fiore (more commonly known as the Duomo) and in 1419 sought an architect to build a dome to cover the massive, 42-meter-wide space above the church's chancel. Such a vast space had not been capped with a dome since the Pantheon's construction, in ancient times.

Brunelleschi won the commission. To overcome this extraordinary architectural challenge, he developed a number of engineering techniques and construction practices. His final design entailed a double-shelled brick dome, with no external buttressing, that rested directly on the church's drum. To complete the design, he invented a unique system of hoists, basing the technology on what he had read the Romans used to construct the Pantheon. His masterpiece defied precedent on innumerable levels: it was the first octagonal dome in history, the first dome to be built without a wooden supporting frame, the largest dome in existence at the time, and is still the largest masonry dome in the world. By drawing on the past and innovating beyond it, Brunelleschi was able to achieve what many had deemed impossible.

What the Renaissance can still teach us

Despite these parallels, there is one important Renaissance innovation practice that rarely figures in today's R&D labs—the use of rivalry. It is difficult to overstate the extent to which the Renaissance was built on the professional rivalries of its major figures. While these men generally held one another in deep respect and esteem, they also competed passionately against one another for commissions, recognition, and prestige. Although competition can sometimes yield petulance and destructive energy, rivalry during the Renaissance seems to have contributed to a competitive culture that bred creativity and innovation. Artists were rivals—but they were also colleagues and frequently friends. To compete, they borrowed from one another, drawing on the techniques and innovations that they most admired from their peers.

A more productive kind of rivalry

Rivalry can mean outright competition—a zero-sum contest in which two individuals or teams go head-to-head and one is declared the winner at the expense of the other. But in the Renaissance, rivalry was linked to a second notion, called *paragone*.[7] In direct translation, *paragone* means "comparison." During the Renaissance, it implied the placing of two artists, or their individual works, side by side in order to judge them, weigh them, distinguish them, and critique them. With *paragone*, two equal rivals were compared and celebrated for their relative achievements. Comparing two or more works in this way did not diminish one at the expense of the other. In fact, artists were sometimes commissioned to work on similar projects simultaneously, with each one presenting a subject in his own unique and brilliant way.

An integral part of the philosophy of *paragone* was the belief that such direct comparison could motivate artists to greater feats. For example, in 1515 the young Raphael was commissioned by Pope Leo X to design ten tapestries for the lower walls of the Sistine Chapel. Knowing they would hang directly below the ceiling painted by Michelangelo, Raphael pushed himself to new heights of creative brilliance.[8]

Harnessing rivalry today

There are few examples of companies that embrace anything approaching *paragone* in their R&D labs. To be sure, some companies hold innovation competitions, such as Tata Group's recent Innovista challenge, which generated 1,700 innovative ideas from across the company. But these onetime contests do not really replicate the kind of productive

[7] Rona Goffen, *Renaissance Rivals: Michelangelo, Leonardo, Raphael, Titian*, New Haven, CT: Yale University Press, 2004.
[8] Marcia B. Hall, ed., *Rome: Artistic Centers of the Italian Renaissance*, New York: Cambridge University Press, 2005.

artistic rivalry that made the Renaissance so creative. Moreover, competition is generally discouraged in the business literature on innovation. Management experts prefer to talk about cooperation and collaboration within R&D centers rather than competition and rivalry.

But rivalry does not necessarily preclude collaboration; we believe R&D managers should be seeking to integrate the two more deeply—in short, to implement a modern form of *paragone*. The best way to do so is to set two or more teams to work on the same project at the same time. Again, this isn't a new idea: recall the famous competition between the System 360 mainframe computer and the 8000 series at IBM during the early 1960s.[9] And as Mark Little, director of General Electric's Global Research Group, explains in the article that follows (see "Competition and collaboration in General Electric's Global Research Group"), his company makes extensive, though understated, use of competition. What we are suggesting is that the idea of competition—specifically, *paragone*— should be a part of more companies' regular R&D processes. This may sound costly, but assigning several teams to tackle the same problem is not necessarily unproductive or inefficient if it leads to *better* solutions. Here are three principles for executives interested in harnessing the power of *paragone*:

Forming teams

Competing teams could come from different divisions, include a diverse array of experts, and take explicitly different approaches to the same problem. After all, there are often many ways (sometimes coming out of different disciplines) to resolve an R&D challenge, and there is often no way of knowing which one is best without trying them out. Moreover, teams can have biases and narrow specializations, making it all the more important to have an explicit diversity of approaches.

Appreciating differences

During the Renaissance, paintings were placed side by side so that viewers could compare and appreciate them and other artists could borrow from them. In the same way, the various solutions that teams develop can be held up next to one another in order to judge them on their relative merits. On many occasions, ideas from one can be integrated into the other. Or a solution that is ultimately passed over can be sent back to the labs for development in new directions.

[9] For more on this competition, see Rowena Olegario, "IBM and the two Thomas J. Watsons," (especially p. 388) in Thomas K. McCraw, ed., *Creating Moden Capitalism*, Cambridge, MA: Harvard University Press, 1997.

Conducting 'market tests'

Another way to replicate the practice of *paragone* is to bring designs to an internal jury or group of customers and let them weigh and contrast the different solutions. In some cases, more than one of the products may find customers who appreciate them, just as Renaissance artists each had their own following.

Whatever the judgment mechanism, there is good reason to believe that having two or more teams working on a given project can have a strong motivational impact. A friendly and healthy degree of rivalry will spur teams to think deeper and harder about a given problem, leading to new levels of creativity. As long as this spirit of rivalry is managed effectively, R&D teams will push themselves further just knowing that their proposals will ultimately be held up in comparison to others.

All that said, we are realistic about the challenges associated with rivalry. Even during the Renaissance, some rivalries grew out of control and at times led to duels, imprisonments, and murders. We have no doubt that poorly managed rivalry could devolve into the kind of destructive competitiveness that R&D managers try to avoid, stifling the exchange of ideas and undermining collaboration. Strong management, though, should be able to ensure that competition does not create bitterness, promote discord, or cause individuals to feel threatened or defensive.

Most important, a company must supplement the implementation of *paragone* with a deep and pervasive culture of cooperation and collective achievement. The Renaissance masters knew that their greatest achievements were probably those that they would accomplish collectively. They wanted nothing less than to define a new age of art, culture, and civilization—and they were never going to do this alone. Likewise, a great company will make sure its innovators understand that its most lasting breakthroughs and achievements are the product of a collective effort—and will celebrate and reward all who participate.

●   ●   ●

Without knowing it, the world's most creative companies have fruitfully embraced many practices that made the Renaissance uniquely creative. Executives who want to push their R&D teams to greater heights might consider drawing from the Renaissance philosophy of *paragone*. Harnessing the creative energy of productive rivalry should yield more, and more valuable, business innovation. ○

Executive perspective:
Mark Little

Competition and collaboration in General Electric's Global Research Group

The head of General Electric's Global Research Group describes how his company uses rivalry to stimulate innovation without disrupting a culture of collaboration.

To get a reality check on the notion that the Italian Renaissance holds valuable insights for executives hoping to stimulate innovation, McKinsey alumnus Bernie Ferrari sat down with GE senior vice president Mark Little, the director of the company's Global Research Group. GE Global Research employs 2,800 people in four research centers (Bangalore, India; Munich, Germany; Niskayuna, New York; and Shanghai, China), who provide basic research and core technology support for the company as a whole. While GE has thousands more technologists spread across its individual businesses, Global Research pursues fundamental innovations in ten technology areas—ranging from biosciences and imaging to ceramic and metallurgy technologies—that cut across GE's business units.

Little's verdict: "It's an interesting thing that you're onto here," he said of the idea that rivalry is an important but often-overlooked lever for catalyzing innovation. A variety of GE research efforts employ rivalry, but Little noted that it is infrequently discussed and often plays second fiddle to collaboration as a cultural norm. Little also described the way in which GE embraces several other Renaissance practices—giving people space, setting stretch goals, encouraging collision between diverse specialists—that are more representative of mainstream R&D approaches.

Productive rivalries

This article was stimulating for me. I hadn't thought much about, or verbalized, rivalry as an element of what we do. But some of my colleagues laughed when I said, "We are sisterhood and brotherhood; we are collaboration; we are teamwork." My colleagues said, "These are scientists. They know how to compete. They know a lot about rivalry." What's interesting, though, is that we don't talk about rivalry. I don't get in front of our people and say, "I love that we've separated you into different teams and that we're playing you off against one another." We don't talk about ourselves as an internally fighting team, although we have a number of processes that do just that. And we don't talk about individual or team success, although we foster it.

What we talk about is working together, collaboration, and the success of our businesses; we want everybody focused on that. Rivalry takes place in an atmosphere of trying to produce results together. Often we'll say, "Please champion this because we need to have this idea sorted out"—not, "You champion this thing, and you're personally bound up in it." It's less personal if I say, "You guys look at A; you guys look at B. You tell us all about A; you tell us all about B. And then we'll sort it out." Whether A or B wins, these teams will come together to make it a success. Here are some real examples of how that works:

Aircraft engines

My colleagues in GE's aviation business reminded me that the GE90—the big, very-high-thrust engine developed back in the 1990s for the Boeing 777—was developed by two independent teams. Now, we would never build two engines and then run them off, because that's just too expensive; you don't spend a billion dollars each on two engines and then test them. But we did have two independent teams do very detailed conceptual designs, and then we ran them off against each other. One of my colleagues was deeply involved; his team won the competition, and then the other team was charged with challenging and pushing everything my colleague's team was doing. He didn't like it, but he said it made them a lot better and helped the whole thing go forward.

Composite materials

Ceramic matrix composites are an emerging technology for very lightweight aircraft engine components that, unlike any metal, can sustain very high temperatures. You want to go to high temperatures in aircraft engines because the higher the air intake temperature, the better efficiency you get out of the system. Our aviation business had one approach; the GE Research Center had a different one. They developed them in parallel, took them down the road, all the way through testing, and then picked one; now we're going forward on that one.

Power generation

Combustion systems for gas turbines are hugely important. There are big differences between peak and off-peak demand, especially in today's world where you have renewables coming off- and on-line, and it's really important to be able to turn gas turbines down. You want to be able to hold the efficiency up while you turn the power down, but machines don't naturally work that way. So we are, as we speak, running off three different technologies, created by three different teams, which are looking at different ways of solving that problem, with interesting, novel technologies. The best team will win, and we will blend the best features of each.

Solar energy

We have had three parallel tracks for solar energy. One is silicon based, which we have really pulled back on because there's a great deal of capacity in that segment, and it's suffering. Then there's thin-film solar, where we've got a little company called PrimeStar Solar that we're injecting research technology into as aggressively as we can. And while working on that, we're working on the next generation of solar energy with another material called CIGS.[1] So we've in effect been competing with three different approaches, run by three different teams, to see which wins in the marketplace.

We have many more examples of this kind of competition going on all over the company: limiting particulate emissions in our transportation business, creating a new battery business, and new imaging approaches in health care. These problems that we're trying to solve are so difficult that, typically, we can't have one person do it. So there's no da Vinci, no Michelangelo making a sculpture on his own. It's a different sort of team game. It's not as if we don't have people who are preeminent leaders in some of these areas, who get to champion those causes. Not at all— we have many of those. We have chief scientists and chief engineers who, in some sense, are like master artists. But they are singular in their discipline. We don't have two in one place. So you don't have rivalry that's directly comparable to that of the master artists.

Making rivalry work

I don't focus on people winning and losing. I focus on people sorting out the pluses and minuses of different options. That's a big, vitally important contribution. I think our scientists and technologists see it that way too. And I have never heard anybody complain about us doing these things.

Of course, that organizational dynamic depends in a significant way on having competent people judge these competitions. If you have somebody in a decision-making position who is viewed, particularly by the losing team, as not really capable of making good technical assessments—say, a manager who is more of a generalist than the deep specialists on the team—that's organizationally bad. So we have mechanisms to guard against that, not the least of which is getting outside people who are experts in on the judgment.

Also, it's not like we say, "We've got a chapel that needs to be painted." We say, "We'd like to do something in oil and gas, and it's this kind of a problem." Then we work with the people who know enough about it to figure out where we should be going. Let's say a team working on battery life is making good progress on the chemistry. We might say, "You know,

---

[1]Copper indium gallium (di)selenide solar cells.

the chemistry isn't going to be enough; we need to work on the configuration too. And we know a person who is brilliant at configuration; let's challenge that person to put together a team." That really happened in this battery case, and it's not uncommon.

Giving researchers space

By and large, our model is to keep people focused on things that they and we together have chosen to work on. We don't say, "Go do whatever you dream about; we will try to find a way to fit it into GE." We say, "These are the spaces that GE is in. These are things that we're interested in learning about. We'd like your ideas on how to solve these kinds of problems or on getting into adjacent kinds of things." For example, because we're not a semiconductor business, we're not asking people to come up with ideas for new semiconductors—even though we have people who are well capable of doing that.

 We don't talk about ourselves as an internally fighting team, although we have a number of processes that do just that. And we don't talk about individual or team success, although we foster it.

Mark Little is director of General Electric's Global Research Group.

Having said that, some of our cooler ideas have come from people dreaming up things on their own and then saying, "Let's look at this idea." And we do have pools of money for seeding ideas. We fund the idea a little bit, we find out we like it, and we fund it more. What we're hoping to do is get these ideas to blossom to the point where the businesses become interested, pick them up, fund them, and turn them into products. It's not people individually sitting around having a lot of free time to do whatever they want to do. But there's a process to get them access to money, which gives them flexibility to do more. That's very much part of how we get new ideas.

Stretch goals

Our people don't come to us to think about the next little incremental thing. So the very nature of the research center is that we're working on things that are hard to do, where the likelihood of failure is not zero. And we also have some overarching goals, a few big themes where we said, "Let's have these be areas where we try to achieve some great things." They are long-term, difficult problems.

One example is solar power. We say we want to get the cost of generating solar electricity to be competitive with the cost of electricity from fossil fuels. Just to give you some context about how hard that is to do, with today's low gas prices, you could probably generate natural gas–fired electricity at 5 or 6 cents a kilowatt hour. Solar costs 25 to 30 cents. Closing that gap is really tough. You don't have to close it all the way, because you can put solar panels on your home and avoid the transmission and distribution costs, which might be another 7 or 8 cents. But it's a big challenge. So we are trying, on multiple fronts, to drive the cost of solar way down.

Another goal is cutting the cost of desalination in half. Another is going to subsea oil and gas and liberating all kinds of new fuel sources that we can't get at today. We also are focused on a couple of kinds of cancer. These are big thematic things. They don't catch everything we do, but they are out there as emblematic goals for us; everybody knows about them, and lots of different people are working on them.

Collision of people and ideas

This place is designed to foster the deep technical excellence that you get by having people come together across disciplines; that's the magic we have. A specific example of this is in health care. We bought Amersham

Biosciences some years back, not very long after starting our own biosciences activity. The Amersham acquisition put us into medical diagnostics in a whole different way. And although Amersham had a research center in New Jersey, it moved its people from New Jersey to Niskayuna.[2] They didn't do that because they thought we had better biologists than they did. They did it because they wanted access to other disciplines: the engineers, the physicists, the device people. The "collision," they knew, would bring them benefits. And it has paid off beautifully.

Another very live and real thing for us is that our business leaders come to the research center routinely. For example, John Dineen, the head of GE Healthcare, spends a full day with us every quarter. To some extent, those sessions are about reviewing the projects we have under way. But in a more important way, they're about shaping the future of the business. These are deep, meaningful discussions, involving serious give and take, that really help shape where we're going. I've heard business leaders say these are their best days at GE, because they are out of the flow of the urgent stuff they typically have to deal with—closing a quarter, winning an order—and are free to really think about the future of their business.

Finally, there is something we call a Session T. Session T is by design a very deep session with customers, most often but not always held at a GE research center. Customers come in and join with people from the GE business that serves them—typically, marketing, product management, and technologists—as well as our people. The purpose of that session is to gather information from the customers about what they see for themselves in the future—what needs they have—and then to think together about how to create what they'd like to have but don't. That's very powerful for us. ○

[2] Niskayuna, New York, is the largest and oldest GE Global Research center of activity.

Picture This

India's urban transformation

The population of India's cities will increase from 340 million in 2008 to 590 million by 2030

Percentage of total population living in cities, by state

- ● 40–70%
- ● 20–39%
- ● <20%
- ○ Cities with populations of 4 million or more

2008

Delhi

Ahmedabad

Surat

Mumbai (MMR[1])
Pune

Hyderabad

Kolkata

Bangalore

Chennai

What's at stake

By 2030, the number of cities with populations of more than 1 million will grow to 68, from the current 42. India's cities could generate **70%** of net new jobs, **70%** of India's GDP, and drive a fourfold increase in per capita incomes.

What it will take

India will need to invest $1.2 trillion in capital expenditure—equivalent to $115 per capita per year—in its cities over the next 20 years. In 2007, India's per capita capital expenditure on urban services was only $17. More than half of the capital investment is necessary to erase India's infrastructure backlog and the rest to finance cities' future needs.

By 2030, India must build 700–900 million square miles of commercial and residential space, equivalent to a new Chicago every year—**cost: $395 billion;** construct 7,400 kilometers of metros and subways—**cost: $392 billion;** pave 2.5 billion square miles of roads—**cost: $199 billion;** and invest **$96 billion** to increase the water supply and an additional **$100 billion** to improve the treatment of sewage.

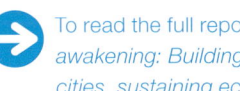

To read the full report, *India's urban awakening: Building inclusive cities, sustaining economic growth,* visit mckinsey.com/mgi.

113

2030

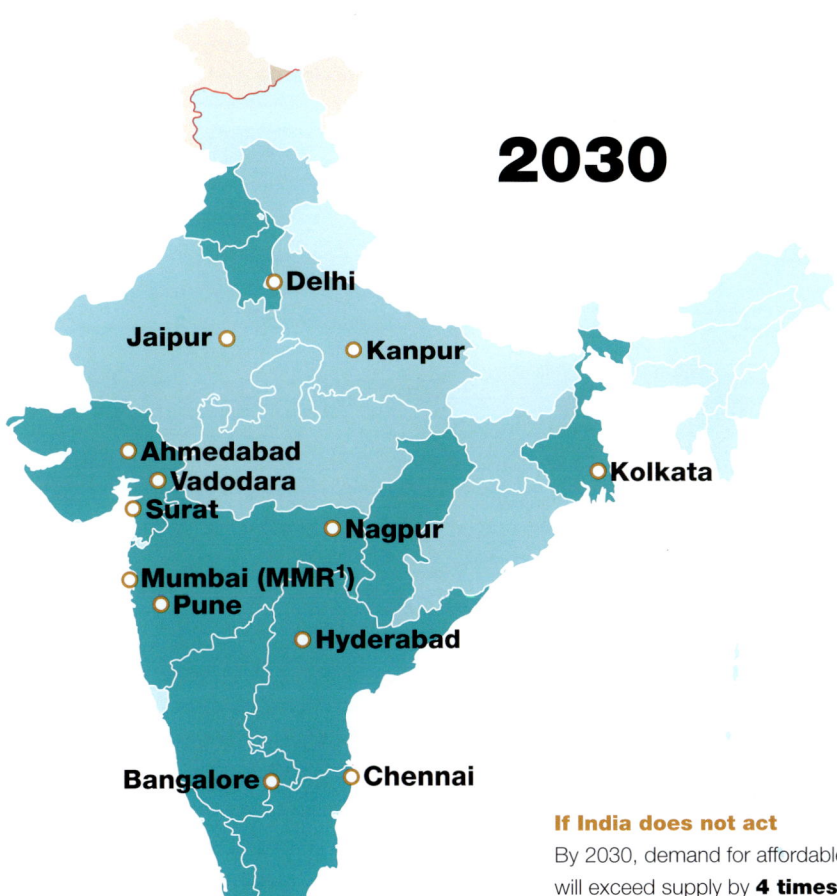

If India does not act

By 2030, demand for affordable housing will exceed supply by **4 times;** demand for rail-based mass transit will be **2.5 times the supply;** demand for private transportation will be **double the supply;** water demand will be **double the supply;** demand for sewage treatment will be **3.5 times the supply.** ○

[1] Mumbai Metropolitan Region.

Richard Dobbs, Shirish Sankhe, and Ireena Vittal

Richard Dobbs is a director in McKinsey's Seoul office; Shirish Sankhe is a director in the Mumbai office, where Ireena Vittal is a principal.

Applied Insight

Tools, techniques, and frameworks for managers

Traffic on the streets of Beijing.

© Redlink Production/Corbis

Applying global trends: A look at China's auto industry

Filipe Barbosa, Damian Hattingh, and Michael Kloss

Strategists can challenge conventional wisdom and better prepare for uncertainty by analyzing the complex and not-so-obvious ways global trends interact in their industries.

Predicting the future is arguably the most important and hardest task facing strategists. One way of loading the dice in their favor: scrutinizing the demographic, technological, environmental, macroeconomic, and other long-term forces constantly shaping the global economy. The most eye-opening implications typically lurk at the intersections where multiple trends (and dozens or more subtrends) interact with one another, often in complex and not-so-obvious ways. Moreover, to analyze trends successfully, executives must develop a fine-grained understanding of the potential impact for specific geographies and industries.[1]

Only a dozen years ago, for example, authoritative predictions for the coming decade envisioned no more than a few million mobile-phone users throughout Africa. Local income, consumption, technology, infrastructure, and regulatory conditions seemed to hold little promise for significant growth. Less than ten years later, though, Nigeria alone had 42 million mobile subscribers— 80 times more than initial forecasts predicted—as growth skyrocketed, largely as a result of the interaction between just two trends: improved income levels and cheaper handsets. This was a massive growth opportunity that global telcos missed but African and Middle Eastern players captured, to the tune of more than $100 billion,[2] by developing low-cost business models.

How can company strategists spot the next big opportunity or looming threat in their industries before it's apparent to everyone? In this article, we'll describe a four-step methodology for making global trends part of a scenario-based strategic-planning process. By bringing together trends and their interactions, industry-specific insights, and problem-solving techniques, this approach helps create quantitative, actionable, and unbiased scenarios for what might happen in the next five to ten years. Better scenarios, in turn, can help companies challenge conventional wisdom, pressure-test existing business models, identify market opportunities, and develop more innovative products and services.

To illustrate our thinking, we'll look at an intriguing example—how Chinese automakers could defy conventional wisdom and steal a march on competitors in developed markets by succeeding there much more quickly than expected in a future characterized by natural-resource constraints, unceasing innovation, a growing role for governments, and a shift of economic growth and power to emerging markets.

[1] See Mehrdad Baghai, Sven Smit, and S. Patrick Viguerie, "The granularity of growth," mckinseyquarterly.com, May 2007.

[2] From 1999 to 2009, the market capitalization of the top five Middle Eastern and African telecom operators increased tenfold, to more than $100 billion.

1. Establish the reference frame

The right frame of reference—a specific problem statement and a clear sense of the industry context for long-term shifts—is a critical starting point. For example: "What share of the car market in developed countries is Chinese auto manufacturers likely to capture by 2020, and what impact could they have on global profit pools?" This might be a timely question for the planning team at a European or US automaker. After all, Chinese automakers enjoy a 35 percent cost advantage over those in developed markets, and Chinese OEMs have supersized ambitions. *BusinessWeek* reported in July 2008, for instance, that Geely Automobile "intends to sell 2 million cars [in the US market] by 2015, and [the CEO is] confident he can thrive against global competition."[3] The company's March 2010 acquisition of Sweden's Volvo Cars suggests that these ambitions aren't just cheap talk.

Still, China's light-vehicle manufacturers haven't entered European or US markets at any scale, nor are they expected to do so soon. IHS Global Insight recently forecast that China's share of these markets would double, from 0.1 percent today to a still-marginal 0.2 percent by 2020. Chinese cars also suffer from poor consumer perceptions of their quality and safety. Evaluations by the China New Car Assessment Program (C-NCAP, a government-supported agency) give the country's automakers a quality index score of around 30, versus 45 for automakers in developed markets.

Hyundai provides a memorable and recent example of an Asian automaker that entered the US market (in the late 1980s) with quality problems and with volumes comparable to those of some smaller Chinese OEMs now. Though quite successful today, it took the company nearly two decades to establish a meaningful presence in developed markets by competing on price and slowly building out its sales network while improving its quality and brand image. Interestingly, the low market share numbers some forecasters expect for China's automakers seem to imply a trajectory similar to Hyundai's in the late 1980s.

But how relevant is this example for today's Chinese automakers? The vast difference in scale between China's domestic auto markets and South Korea's is obvious. But Chinese market penetration might be similarly measured if certain conditions held sway—such as the absence of major technological breakthroughs in engine technology, continued quality problems for Chinese automakers, and a need for the slow, steady development of a sales network.

[3]Dexter Roberts, "China's Geely has global auto ambitions," *BusinessWeek*, July 17, 2008.

Chinese automakers enjoy a **35 percent** cost advantage over those in developed markets.

2. Expand the solution space

Having carefully defined the problem and the industry context surrounding it, the challenge for strategists is to broaden the potential solution space by challenging conventional wisdom through the lens of global trends. Most companies have a broad range of experts who can help, yet these people are often tucked away in organizational silos that make it difficult for them to connect the dots. Automakers in the developed world are very good at gathering rich trend data and perspectives on topics such as regulation, macroeconomics, and demand. But regulatory analysts in car companies may spend more time developing strategies for government relations and lobbying than they do working with internal economists forecasting future demand. Those economists, in turn, rarely interact with engineers who focus on future game-changing technological possibilities.

[4] BYD Auto, an upstart automaker that began as a supplier of batteries and electronic components to mobile-phone makers, recently announced that it will have an electric car for the US market in 2011.

When companies overcome these and other strategic and organizational barriers, they can begin developing a rigorous and more nuanced picture of how trends and subtrends might influence their industries. In the auto industry, for instance, could the developing world's rising economic influence, the increasing scarcity of resources, and the spread of "green" technologies combine to affect the market, with unexpected results?

While events could play out in many ways, Chinese carmakers could well leapfrog current engine technology and develop a significant competitive advantage in electric vehicles or other clean technologies; the Chinese player BYD Auto appears to be moving in this direction already.[4] For one thing, global resource constraints are prompting China to reduce its dependence on foreign oil, as well as pollution and greenhouse gas

A man charges a BYD Auto electric vehicle at the company's campus in Shenzhen, China.

© Bloomberg/Getty Images

emissions. With large funds available through an economic-stimulus package, the Chinese government is already investing significantly in R&D for alternative technologies.

In parallel, China's massive buildup of new infrastructure might spark an entirely novel green automotive infrastructure, without the massive replacement costs developed nations would incur. This infrastructure could include service networks and promote incentives for clean-tech cars (say, special traffic lanes and preferential parking). Such moves might inspire a large-scale consumer preference for alternative-technology vehicles, allowing Chinese automakers to achieve the required scale to begin mass production; China, remember, is a homogenous automotive market—as well as the world's largest and fastest-growing one. This, in turn, would give China's carmakers a cost and knowledge advantage that might help them pass over competitors in the developed world.

Likewise, Chinese cars could rapidly exceed minimum quality and safety standards if the government's appetite for technology and management know-how drove it to support the acquisition of a major automaker in a developed market (say, one of the top five). This move would speed the transfer of best practices to local Chinese companies, thus helping them to move rapidly up the learning curve, to improve their brand image, and to develop a more sophisticated understanding of consumer needs. Alternately, the Chinese government might raise safety, emission, and quality standards in response to consumer demands while simultaneously subsidizing local players so that they could meet the more stringent requirements.

Finally, natural-resource constraints and environmental concerns might persuade consumers in developed markets to adopt cost-effective clean-tech vehicles more quickly than expected, creating a large market that Chinese auto players would be poised to supply.

3. Define scenarios

In broadening the solution space by highlighting the way trends may interact to challenge conventional wisdom, we've emphasized two variables that seem quite uncertain and will probably have a major impact on the industry's evolution: first, whether Chinese manufacturers can achieve a scale advantage in clean technology and, second, whether they will acquire a large, leading Western auto brand. We can use these two variables to generate a handful of scenarios, each with a compelling but distinct narrative. A methodology called "quadrant crunching," which the US Central

Intelligence Agency developed in recent years, allows planners to generate extreme but plausible scenarios quickly by reversing their underlying assumptions to arrive at a number of very different potential states of the world. This approach can help business strategists combine uncertainties to provide a basis for robust, quantitative, and therefore actionable scenarios, such as the following for our Chinese automotive example:

• A perfect storm. China's government aggressively promotes its carmakers by creating the conditions for a domestic clean-tech market to flourish and by helping a Chinese company buy a major automotive business in a developed market in order to facilitate rapid market entry.

- **The clean-tech advantage.** China's market for clean-tech vehicles flourishes, allowing domestic automakers to develop competitive advantages to compete head-on in developed markets, but without acquiring a brand in any of them.

- **A helping hand.** A Chinese acquisition of a top auto player (one much larger than Volvo) in a developed market combines established brands and quality perceptions with access to a large sales network, as well as a homegrown cost advantage in traditional vehicles powered by combustion engines.

- **Follow in Hyundai's footsteps.** Chinese auto players use their existing brands or create new ones, leveraging their factor cost advantage to produce inexpensive traditional cars that compete head-on with the cars of incumbents in developed markets.

Two uncertainties could have a major impact on the evolution of China's auto industry and can be used to define potential scenarios.

Four 2020 scenarios, estimated Chinese auto OEMs' market share and capture of profit pool[1] in developed markets

		The clean-tech advantage Market share: **3–6%** Profit pool: **$1 billion–$3 billion**	**A perfect storm** Market share: **7–15%** Profit pool: **$4 billion–$8 billion**
Variable 1: Chinese OEMs develop significant scale advantages in clean tech	Yes No	**Following in Hyundai's footsteps** Market share: **0–3%** Profit pool: **0–$1 billion**	**A helping hand** Market share: **3–6%** Profit pool: **$1 billion–$3 billion**
		No	Yes

2 methods to estimate the probability of each scenario and market share impact
- Quantitative analysis where trends are well-established and predictable
- Delphi technique[2] where outcomes are binary (either/or), difficult to predict, or both

Variable 2: Chinese OEMs acquire 1 or more major developed-market OEMs

The clean-tech advantage	**Following in Hyundai's footsteps**	**A helping hand**	**A perfect storm**
Chinese OEMs leapfrog technologies to develop first compelling electric car	Chinese OEMs compete head-on in developed markets	Chinese OEMs buy top auto player, combining established brand/quality with cost advantage	China aggressively promotes OEMs by heavily subsidizing clean tech and buying established brands

[1] Assumes Chinese OEMs achieve profitability similar to that of current compact segment average.
[2] Systematic forecasting method developed in the 1940s to minimize groupthink. It draws on knowledge of panel of experts with diverse, incomplete information.

4. Quantify industry impact

Such scenarios are important because they provide strategic clarity, and they become even more powerful when accompanied by probabilities and financial estimates that help clarify their implications. One classic approach involves the Delphi technique—a systematic forecasting method, developed in the 1940s, that draws on the knowledge of a panel of experts with diverse, incomplete information. By keeping individual predictions anonymous and using an iterative process to converge on a limited set of outcomes, this method minimizes "groupthink" and helps experts to get comfortable with high levels of uncertainty.

We used the Delphi method with a panel of McKinsey auto industry experts after briefing them extensively on the scenarios. The outcome? The panelists saw only a 40 percent likelihood that the scenario based on conventional wisdom would be realized. In this scenario, Chinese automotive companies would capture, at most, $1 billion of the profit pool in developed markets by 2020.

By contrast, the panel saw a 60 percent likelihood of an aggressive entry by China into developed markets, with Chinese players capturing a 3 to 15 percent market share. One scenario gave Chinese players a

The Delphi technique

A systematic forecasting method developed in the 1940s, this method draws on the knowledge of a panel of experts with diverse, incomplete information to generate predictions on which future scenarios can be based.

Stages	Design	Quality control	Run the poll	Synthesize
	Design the panel, choose the questions, and identify the panelists.	Double-check the panel's composition and scrutinize questions.	Poll, aggregate responses, repoll.	Aggregate the final estimates.
Imperatives	Ask the panelists for estimates, justification, and level of confidence in their estimate. Choose panelists with a general background but with knowledge spike.	Be sure the panel is balanced. Do a dry run with team members or colleagues to be sure questions are clear.	Group the justifications and aggregate predictions. Repoll until the estimates don't change (2–3 times should be enough).	Look for the story between the justifications and the estimates. Weigh the estimates by self-assessed confidence levels.
Caveats	Avoid ambiguous questions, which confuse panelists and result in unusable answers.	Avoid a preponderance of like-minded panelists by including external experts. Homogeneity among panelists may lend a perception of rigor to a biased estimate.	Results will often cluster around scenarios. Don't allow the story to be effaced, but do average the results.	Don't report on the precision of the forecast (eg, confidence intervals); rather, include average confidence of each group of panelists.

10 to 15 percent chance of entering the developed world with the benefits of both a clean-tech cost advantage and a major acquisition. Subsequently, we estimated that this scenario implies that Chinese automakers would capture a whopping $4 billion to $7 billion share of the global profit pool.

To be sure, much would have to happen for this most aggressive scenario to play out, but it is plausible enough—and the stakes are high enough—to demand more serious attention from auto strategists in developed markets. Indeed, if this scenario came to pass, the implications would be significant: developed-market players would likely see a big profit erosion that could put their viability in question, thus propelling a large-scale restructuring of the industry.

Uncertainty isn't limited to the auto sector. A wider range of actionable scenarios based on a granular understanding of global trends and their interactions can help strategists in any industry see opportunities where others see only uncertainty. Armed with a more robust outlook, executives can define the appropriate strategic postures, identify no-regrets moves and steps to mitigate risk, and spot the potential big bets—insights that together underpin a long-term strategic plan. By reassessing scenarios over time, companies can prepare to seize opportunities before their competitors do. ○

•   •   •

To read more about harnessing global trends, visit mckinsey.com/strategic_trends.

The authors would like to thank the following people who provided input to this article: Dago Diedrich, Dieter Düsedau, Russell Hensley, Hanns Joachim Krösche, and Stefano Proverbio.

Filipe Barbosa is a principal in McKinsey's Johannesburg office, where Damian Hattingh is a consultant and Michael Kloss is a director. Copyright © 2010 McKinsey & Company. All rights reserved.

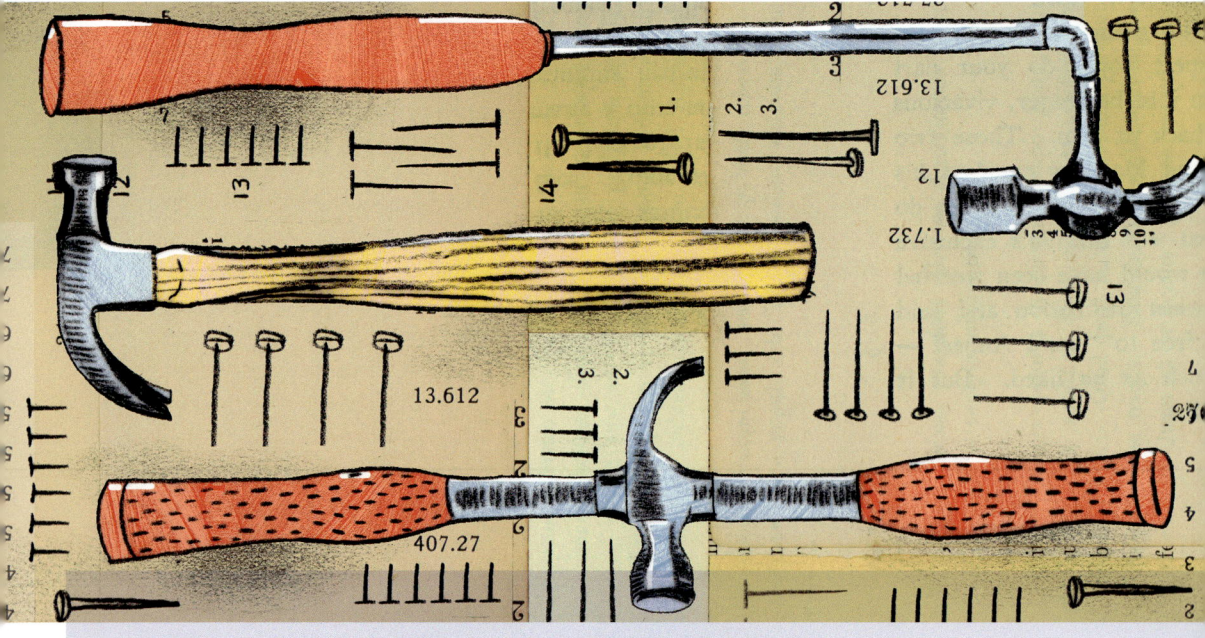

Putting organizational complexity in its place

Julian Birkinshaw and Suzanne Heywood

Not all complexity is bad for business—but executives don't always know what kind their company has. They should understand what creates complexity for most employees, remove what doesn't add value, and channel the rest to employees who can handle it effectively.

Despite widespread agreement that organizational complexity creates big problems by making it hard to get things done, few executives have a realistic understanding of how complexity actually affects their own companies. When pressed, many leaders cite the *institutional* manifestations of complexity they personally experience: the number of countries the company operates in, for instance, or the number of brands or people they manage. By contrast, relatively few executives consider the forms of *individual* complexity that the vast majority of their employees face—for example poor processes, confusing role definitions, or unclear accountabilities.

This is not a trivial difference in perception. Our experience suggests that such a disconnect highlights a blind spot many executives have when it comes to managing complexity effectively. A focus on institutional complexity at the expense of the individual kind can lead to wasted effort or even organizational damage. What's more, failing to tackle complexity as most people experience it can, as we've shown before, be financially costly.[1]

Once senior executives recognize that employees typically see complexity very differently than they do, they can begin to take straightforward steps to pinpoint where in their organizations complexity hinders productivity and why. The goal? To identify where institutional complexity is an issue, where complexity caused by factors such as a lack of

[1] We found that companies reporting low levels of individual complexity had the highest returns on capital employed and returns on invested capital. For more, see Suzanne Heywood, Jessica Spungin, and David Turnbull, "Cracking the complexity code," mckinseyquarterly.com, May 2007.

role clarity or poor processes is a problem, and what's responsible for the complexity in each area. Companies can then boost organizational effectiveness through a combination of two things: removing complexity that doesn't add value and channeling what's left to employees who can either handle it naturally or be trained to cope with it.

In this article, we review the experience of a multinational consumer goods manufacturer that applied this approach in several regions and functions and consequently halved the time it needed to make decisions in critical processes. This, in turn, helped it bring products to market faster in response to changing customer needs. Such payoffs aren't unusual. Our work with companies in the banking, mining, retail, and other sectors suggests that managing complexity more effectively helps remove unnecessary costs and organizational friction and can even lead to new sources of profit and competitive advantage by boosting a company's resilience and its ability to adapt quickly.

Executives at the manufacturer knew they had a problem with complexity. Rapid growth in the company's

Australasia region was requiring significant management attention and travel time and, consequently, was making it difficult for the senior team to manage effectively there and across the company's two other regions (Europe and the United States).

For most employees, however, such institutional complexity didn't matter. They struggled instead with forms of individual complexity— for example, processes that had initially been effective but over time had become increasingly bureaucratic. Many employees, for instance, were frustrated both with how long it took for decisions to filter through to the front line and the amount of work required to implement them (new-product development, for example, took more than a year and required numerous consultations across the company). Duplicated roles (the regions replicated activities performed by the corporate center) and unclear role definitions, which left several groups accountable for sales forecasting and other key activities, only exacerbated the problems. The result was too much time spent on managing internal processes and not enough on understanding customers' needs.

Survey the scene

To take stock of the situation, the manufacturer launched a survey that asked employees about the clarity of roles and accountabilities across the company, whether systems and processes were linked effectively, how much coordination individual jobs required and how predictable they were, and, very simply, how

hard it was for individuals to get things done and to make decisions.

Although surveys like this are a relatively straightforward way to collect useful information, structured interviews or focus groups are also effective for gathering quantitative data about the intensity of complexity and qualitative information on what drives it. Companies can also make a first assessment simply by looking at their own organization charts with fresh eyes. If, for example, employees report that role duplication is a problem, executives can examine job descriptions and org charts to better determine the likely extent of duplication and follow up with the appropriate managers to learn more.

Likewise, companies can uncover hidden pockets of complexity by interviewing employees to understand the key activities, data, and handoffs involved in various business processes. Whatever the method of data collection, companies must avoid sampling subsets— say, a single business unit— and assuming that these views are representative.

Draw a map of what's really going on

Armed with the survey data, the manufacturer constructed several "heat maps" to help senior managers pinpoint where and why complexity was causing trouble for employees. Each map showed a particular breakdown—a region or function, for example—and how much complexity of various kinds was occurring there, as well as the level of coping skills employees possessed. The manufacturer's maps helped identify several problems that executives had previously been unaware of.

A heat map revealed how much complexity existed within regions or functions and how well the employees were coping with it.

Sample regional complexity heat map, based on amalgam of employees' responses to a number of questions

■ Most difficult   ■ Moderately difficult   ■ Least difficult

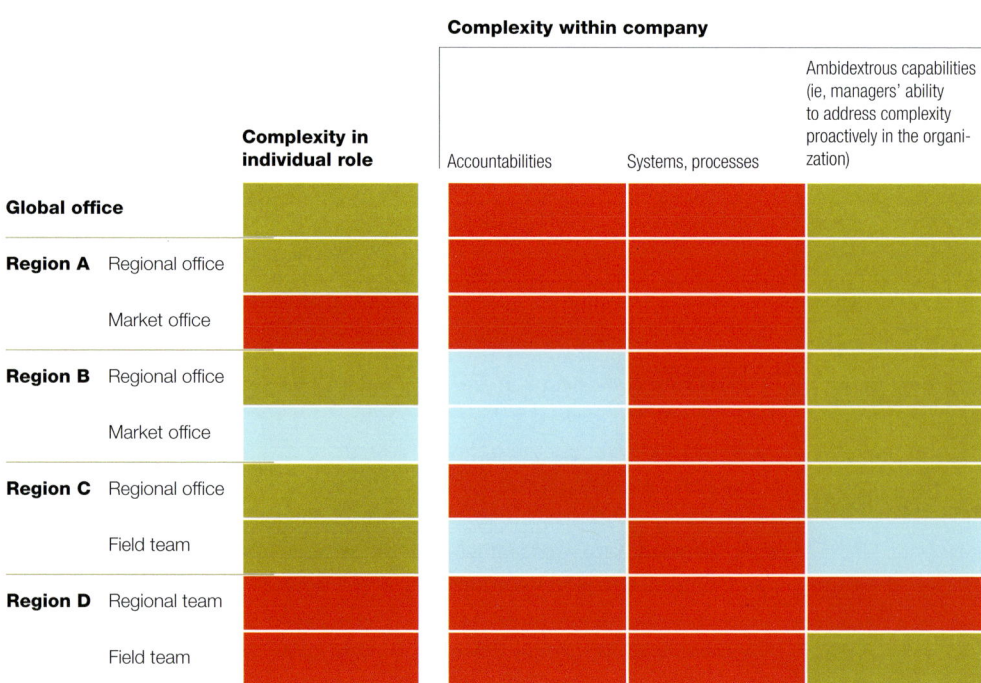

Types of complexity

Imposed complexity includes laws, industry regulations, and interventions by nongovernmental organizations. It is not typically manageable by companies.

Inherent complexity is intrinsic to the business and can only be jettisoned by exiting a portion of the business.

Designed complexity results from choices about where the business operates, what it sells, to whom, and how. Companies can remove it, but this could mean simplifying valuable wrinkles in their business model.

Unnecessary complexity arises from growing misalignment between the needs of the organization and the processes supporting it. Once identified, it is easily managed.

- A regional map, reproduced here, highlighted confusion over accountability between the company's headquarters and a country office in the same region. The country's head of operations found it difficult to get things done because some of the roles in her group were shared with headquarters—her marketing function, for example, also worked for headquarters, while the corporate HR function worked, in part, for her country office. Moreover, the same map showed that employees in Region B found it markedly easier to do their work than employees in Region D did, despite having similar mandates and processes and selling, essentially, the same products.

The reason? Region B's employees had far fewer interactions with headquarters than did their colleagues in Region D.

- Another map showed how the manufacturer's supply chain employees were struggling with duplication that stemmed from confusing sales forecasting and from ordering processes that required decisions to pass through multiple loops (including time-consuming iterations with regional offices) prior to approval. What's worse, a closer look found that the additional checks and inputs weren't improving the accuracy of the forecasts—these efforts were wasted.

- Meanwhile, executives learned that midlevel managers in all the regions were not using the company's performance-management system effectively. This meant both that the performance information collected was not as accurate as it could be and (more important) that the system was being used only for tracking performance against targets and not for coaching or for conducting developmental discussions on skill gaps and how to close them. Poor data, in turn, made it hard to align employees' skills with the manufacturer's overall strategic needs.

Reduce— and redirect— complexity

Once senior managers have a clear picture of where complexity hampers effectiveness, they can begin to remove any complexity that doesn't add value and channel what's left to people who can handle it. Of course, managers must be mindful that not all complexity is equally manageable, and proceed accordingly (see sidebar, "Types of complexity").

For example, to tackle the confusion that had arisen between company headquarters and the country office, the manufacturer redrew its functional boundaries so that marketing and other groups served either the country office or corporate headquarters—but not both. This simplified the jobs of the majority of employees and funneled the necessary interactions between the country office and headquarters to the country managers.

To improve sales and forecasting processes, the manufacturer zeroed in on the information its marketing employees needed most: insights on likely sales volumes given customer needs and the competitive situation. Some insights, it turned out, could be converted into forecasts relatively easily by using data from prior sales periods; others required very specific local input. To provide it, the manufacturer created small teams based in—and focused on—each geographic area. Team members' job descriptions were standardized, and each member was given clear accountabilities for working with headquarters on forecasting, pricing, and promotions. This allowed the manufacturer to remove all unnecessary inputs to the processes, focus local efforts where they were most valuable, and cut the number of rounds of consultations in half.

Meanwhile, the company simplified the sign-off process by building it into its regular business-planning activities, thereby providing more regularity and clarity around the timing of decisions. While these actions added complexity for some workers, the overall level of complexity for most employees dropped markedly, reducing wasted time and frustration while generating forecasts that were just as good as the old ones. Equally important, to prevent unnecessary complexity from returning, the new job descriptions were agreed to globally, and the right to change them was retained by the executive team.

Finally, to tackle the HR problems, the manufacturer put in place a consistent talent review process across the business that focused much more on performance-management conversations and developmental discussions.

Bolster skills where needed

Of course, whenever executives consciously funnel complexity into new locations or "design in" new elements that create added complexity for added reward, they must ensure that the employees in the positions affected are prepared. In many cases, companies will see a need to improve key capabilities in HR and other functional areas.

This was true for the manufacturer, which began addressing its long-term skill gaps by focusing on the recruitment and training of HR employees. At the same time, however, the manufacturer's senior team was careful to provide immediate training to those HR employees who needed help mastering the company's revamped talent review process and rolled out training for all line managers across the business on how they should use this new process to coach and develop staff members—and not just to measure staff performance passively against targets.

Such experiences are common. Whenever companies tackle complexity, they will ultimately find some individuals who seem less troubled by it than others. This is not surprising. People are different: some freeze like deer in the headlights in the face of ambiguity, uncertainty, complex roles, and unclear accountabilities; others are able to get their work done regardless. Companies need to locate the pockets of individual strength and weakness in order to respond intelligently. Although some people can deal with complexity innately, we now know that others can be trained to develop what we call "ambidextrous" capabilities—the ability to tolerate ambiguity and actively manage complexity. Such skills will enable employees to create and use networks within organizations to build relationships and help overcome poor processes, bridge organizational silos, or manage whatever value-creating pockets of complexity their companies decide to maintain.

Organizations aren't uniformly complex, and most employees don't experience complexity the way executives do. To better manage complexity, senior leaders must recognize how employees at all levels see it, and then learn what's driving it. By doing so, companies can retain the kinds of complexity that add value, remove the kinds that don't, and channel the rest to employees, at any level, who can be trained to handle it effectively. o

●   ●   ●

Julian Birkinshaw is a professor at the London Business School; Suzanne Heywood is a principal in McKinsey's London office. Copyright © 2010 McKinsey & Company. All rights reserved.

Readers speak out

We invited mckinseyquarterly.com readers to share their stories of organizational complexity: how complexity arose, how it undermined the effectiveness of their organizations, and how they coped with—or sought to fix—the problem.

....

Anders Eiby-Johannesen

Sales director, Fujitsu, Denmark

In the process of merging two companies, we decided that selected sales individuals should, from then on, bring the new and combined services and product stack to the market. This added complexity, since each side of the merger had limited knowledge of what the other side had to offer. On the one hand, it was clear that certain members of the sales force did not have the necessary competencies and, equally important, did not have the potential and willingness to get them. These people were replaced. On the other hand, some members of the sales force expressed that while they did not have the competencies now, they were very interested in getting them. These people sought increased complexity and were encouraged by it. Looking back at their personnel files, we could also see that they had asked their managers for greater challenges for a long time. For this group, the merger, increased complexity, and subsequent new requirements came as an answer to their prayers.

....

Prakash Bhat

Chartered accountant, Mumbai, India

My experience at a pharmaceuticals company is that existing complexities increase significantly with mergers and acquisitions, and that complexities are of broadly two types: one relating to business—namely, multiple business/SKUs—and a second relating to organization. In both, we observed that many times employees have a vested interest in maintaining the complexity. It gives them comfort and a sense of security.

....

Harold Fethe

Former senior vice president, Alza, Silicon Valley, CA, USA

Alza, bought by Johnson & Johnson in 2001, when our revenue was more than $1 billion, was a highly productive, very complex organization. We had five pharmaceutical technologies, each with multiple products and projects. We purposely had a true, classic matrix organization—with both project managers and function managers—from the founding of the company in the early 1970s, and were among the first to do so. As head of HR, every 24 to 36 months I brought in a matrix organization expert and "big thinker" to evaluate our organization. We rewarded collaborative behavior and recognized that competition for limited resources (budget wrangles, priority debates) actually strengthens the organization if done civilly. And, the most often cited "positive" by departing employees was the culture. You can have constructive conflict; competition for resources; multi-technology, multiproduct complexity; science; government regulation; and a great corporate culture. It just has to start at the top and be reinforced constantly as a "condition of membership."

Gaining an edge through digital marketing

David C. Edelman

Companies that make the deep strategic, organizational, and operational shifts required to become effective digital marketers can be more agile and productive, while also accelerating revenue growth.

Since the dawn of the Internet, marketers have regarded it as a vast laboratory, launching experiment after experiment to generate sales and customer loyalty. Not surprising, most have failed. Consumers adopted digital technology as they saw fit, fundamentally altering the way they make purchasing decisions.[1] Companies that understand this evolution are now carefully moving digital interactivity toward the center of their marketing strategies, rethinking their priorities and budgets, and substantially reshaping their processes and skills.

Through our work with dozens of companies navigating this shifting landscape, we have found that the most successful digital marketers think differently. They view themselves as publishers of online content, not just marketers, and they recognize the opportunity to inspire consumers who will in return become advocates for their products and brands.

Successful digital marketers also act differently. They seek to immerse consumers in their content, investing to deliver an experience that goes beyond a straight transaction. And to ensure that their digital efforts are as effective as possible, they closely monitor what consumers are seeing, doing, and saying.

In our experience, some marketers have made great progress thinking and acting in these new ways, while others have not. But even marketing professionals still in the starting blocks have been exposed more intensively to the transformation in consumer behavior than have executives from outside the marketing function. This article, presenting a view from the digital trenches, is meant to assist nonmarketers in making sense of the changing consumer landscape and to help them work with marketers to establish priorities.

[1] See David Court, Dave Elzinga, Susan Mulder, and Ole Jørgen Vetvik, "The consumer decision journey," mckinseyquarterly.com, June 2009.

Companies should think like publishers, not advertisers.

Embedded costs for a content supply chain can range from $50 million to $75 million for a consumer products OEM to over $300 million for a global technology company.

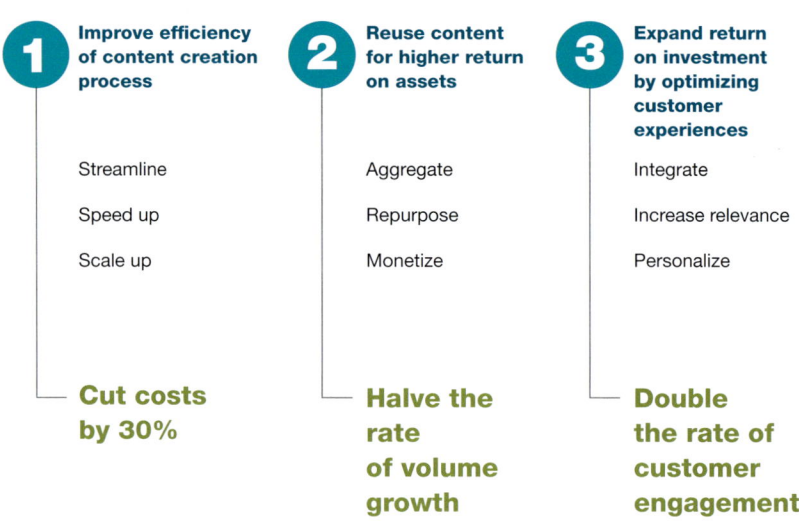

3 avenues for value creation

1 **Improve efficiency of content creation process**

Streamline

Speed up

Scale up

Cut costs by 30%

2 **Reuse content for higher return on assets**

Aggregate

Repurpose

Monetize

Halve the rate of volume growth

3 **Expand return on investment by optimizing customer experiences**

Integrate

Increase relevance

Personalize

Double the rate of customer engagement

Think . . .
....

. . . like a publisher, not an advertiser

Consumers today learn about products and services by reading online reviews, comparing features and prices on Web sites, and discussing options via social networks. Supporting this process requires a vast and growing range of content well beyond advertisements. While many companies chasing digital opportunities have slowly but steadily begun publishing everything from static content (such as product descriptions) to games and other multimedia, most behave like simple advertisers. If they adopted the mind-set of publishers, they could lower costs and eliminate unnecessary duplication, inconsistent content quality, and spotty interactions with customers.

One global business-to-business software provider, for example, produced a growing amount of tailored content—from advertising to cost-of-ownership analytic tools to sales support materials to instruction manuals—for each of its products in every geography. Obsolete content persisted across the Web. Much useful content was poorly tagged or not well-linked to related content, making it hard for consumers to find. Product descriptions on the company's own Web site, for instance, were often different from descriptions of the same products on distributors' sites. Finally, budgets for content creation were buried across business units, and no one had a clear sense of how to pare down the amount of content or raise it to a consistent standard.

For the software company, the solution was to adopt a comprehensive, portfolio-based view of its content and to streamline production costs, make content more reusable, and find new ways to improve the experience the content delivered. The company began by digging into activities across the enterprise to calculate its total publishing costs and understand the spread of its multimedia publishing presence. Then it started to rationalize the system. Acting as a tightly disciplined, personalized publisher helped the company to cut its operating costs by tens of millions of dollars a year and generated more sales leads. Salespeople felt more confident about directing customers to the Web for research and support during the buying process. By improving the customer experience, the new approach improved efficiency and raised returns on assets and investment.

. . . of your customers as marketers

Traditional marketers spend about 60 percent of their budgets on working media (or paid placement), 20 percent on creating content, and the balance on employees and agencies. Digital channels, with their social nature, reverse the economics, focusing on a smaller core of engaged people who can share information and positive impressions with a broader audience.[2]

[2]See Jacques Bughin, Jonathan Doogan, and Ole Jørgen Vetvik, "A new way to measure word-of-mouth marketing," mckinseyquarterly.com, April 2010.

Active digital marketers typically devote about 30 percent of their marketing budgets to paid media and 50 percent to content. Customers do more of the heavy lifting as they decide what to look at, play with content, and forward it to their online communities. Allowing consumers to make brands their own inevitably raises concerns among companies fearful of losing control over brands. The key is striking a balance between retaining control and creating opportunities for consumers to embrace your content. One prominent example is the American Express Members Project. Created to help consumers promote their favorite causes, this initiative offered $5 million to the nonprofit group that garnered the most vociferous support. Despite very limited paid media, this initiative generated an explosive viral campaign that made it one of the company's most successful brand-building efforts.

Act . . .

. . . to help the customer

Few customers today are content merely to watch or read advertisements and then wander into a store for advice from a salesperson. Many customers receive marketing e-mails, search for products online, or use mobile devices to find retail coupons. They continually interact with brands as they move closer to making purchase decisions, and digital channels can unify that experience and prevent the leakage of opportunity. Television commercials should inspire keywords for consumers to search. Great search positioning should offer easy-to-find Web links to specific offers promoted by other media. Links should go deep into specific places to help consumers learn about and buy products. Retailer sites should show exactly the same products, with exactly the same images, rich descriptions, and inventory availability.

A comparable degree of rigor is required to ensure that marketing investments are proportional to the influence they may have on a prospective customer's purchasing decision. Consider the experience of one global consumer product company that traditionally relied on mass-media campaigns when launching new offerings. Because the brand was already well known, the campaigns failed to increase actual sales: the company was spending a disproportionate percentage of its marketing budget on advertising that consumers were largely ignoring.

The company realized that a big shift was needed—one that would likely ripple through much of its budgeting process, organizational structure, and agency lineup. Focusing its spending on efforts to influence consumers as they actually evaluated products, it increased its presence in stores and online, improved its search engine positioning, developed content for retailers' Web sites, and cultivated recommendations from important online influencers, such as bloggers. Traditional-media spending fell, and budgets for advertising agencies shifted toward online-content development. As a result, the company doubled its rate of consideration as a top-three brand, almost tripled the rate of recommendations by salespeople in stores, and increased its market share.

. . . as if information is priceless

When prospective customers actively evaluate their product options, the right message, in the right location, is needed immediately. When online conversations start to trash your brand, no response can be fast enough. When you need to optimize your search and other media spending on ever-faster cycles, there's no time to waste. Savvy digital marketers are therefore mastering intelligence-gathering tools and processes. These tools analyze what customers are seeing, by examining positions in search results or coverage on key retail sites; what customers are doing, by analyzing their online behavior; and what customers are saying, by mining online discus-sions and soliciting ongoing feed-back. This intelligence—the lifeblood of digital leadership—disseminates insights throughout an organization and promotes the personalization needed to help consumers regard a brand as their own.

Companies should develop the ability to assess and utilize customer intel-ligence in real time to drive perform-ance. Dell, for example, has a full-time team that monitors its IdeaStorm discussion boards and rapidly responds to posts. Packaged-goods companies are starting to manage thousands of search terms on a daily basis, not only optimizing what they spend but also looking for keywords customers use in association with their brands. Marketers must

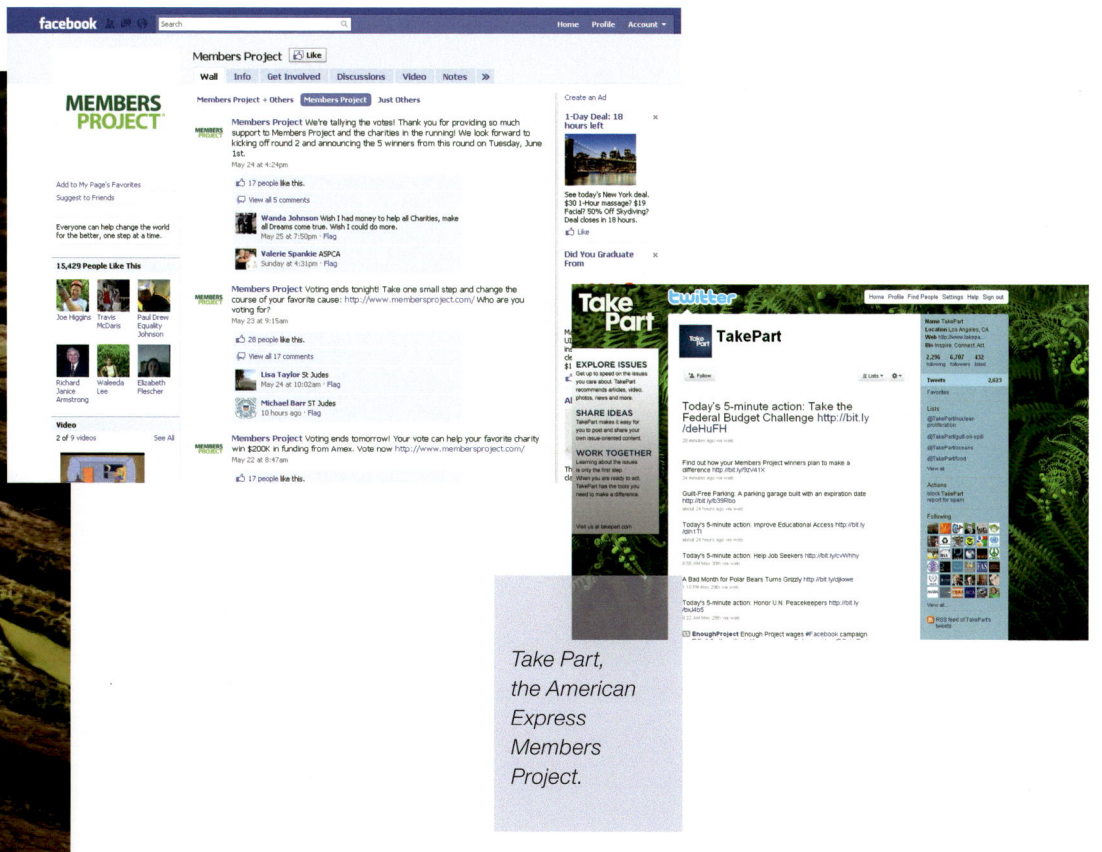

Take Part, the American Express Members Project.

prioritize what to measure, as well as assign a cross-functional team to analyze the data generated. Then they must have clear processes to gather insights, track results, and act.

●   ●   ●

Such issues are too important for executives outside the marketing function to ignore. Questions like the ones below are a helpful starting point for building, across the C-suite, a shared understanding and commitment to change:

- What is the total cost of our digital marketing across the organization, who's responsible for managing our content across channels, and is our publishing well-managed for cost-effectiveness?

- What is our plan—including the people and dollars to be invested—for engaging and nurturing a core group of passionate brand advocates? How do we plan to tap the viral and feedback value they can provide?

- How well does our digital-marketing approach—our content, the links between different channels, and our investment levels—correspond to the way our customers make purchasing decisions?

- What early-warning signs do we track on an ongoing basis to keep ahead of changes in customer behavior, the actions of competitors, and attitudes toward our brand? Who is responsible for acting on what we learn about what our customers see, do, and say?

The answers can help marketing leaders and their senior colleagues in other functions decide whether a company is investing sufficiently in delivering digital messages and what it will need to track the quality and impact of its efforts. Marketing may require more resources, but they should come at a price: greater accountability for sales, innovation, and operational efficiency. Business line executives should demand better visibility into metrics about the delivery of digital messages and greater clarity about how marketing plans will directly improve corporate performance. In return, marketers will generate value as brands become central to helping customers get what they want. o

David Edelman is a principal in McKinsey's Boston office.

Retaining key employees in times of change

Sabine Cosack, Matthew Guthridge, and Emily Lawson

Many companies throw financial incentives at senior executives and star performers during times of change. There is a better and less costly solution.

Too many companies approach the retention of key employees during disruptive periods of organizational change by throwing financial incentives at senior executives, star performers, or other "rainmakers." The money is rarely well spent. In our experience, many of the recipients would have stayed put anyway; others have concerns that money alone can't address. Moreover, by focusing exclusively on high fliers, companies often overlook those "normal" performers who are nonetheless critical for the success of any change effort.

Our work with companies in many sectors (among them, energy, financial services, health care, pharmaceuticals, and retailing) suggests there is a better and less costly approach to employee retention—and one that will serve companies well as they merge, restructure, and reorganize to seize strategic opportunities as the economy picks up. It starts with identifying *all* key players, but targeting only those who are most critical and most at risk of leaving. These people are then offered a mix of financial and nonfinancial incentives tailored to their aspirations and concerns. A European industrial company applied this approach during a recent reorganization and found that it required only 25 percent of the budget that had previously been spent on a broad, cash-based scheme. What follows are three suggestions for companies with similar hopes of keeping their top talent without breaking the bank.

1. Find the "hidden gems"

HR and line managers need to work together during times of major organizational change to identify people whose retention is critical. Yet too often companies simply round up the usual suspects—high-potential employees and senior executives in roles that are critical for business success. Few look in less obvious places for more average performers whose skills or social networks may be critical—both in keeping the lights on during the change effort itself as well as in delivering against its longer-term business objectives.

These "hidden gems" might be found anywhere in the company: for example, the product-development manager in an acquired company's R&D function who is nearing retirement age and no longer on the company's list of "high potentials"—yet who is crucial to ensuring a healthy product pipeline; or the key financial accountant responsible for consolidating the acquired company's next financial report. Even if the employees' performance and career potential are unexceptional, their institutional knowledge, direct relationships, or technical expertise can make their retention critical. In one merger we recently observed, certain sales support personnel who filled orders and took inventory turned out to be just as important as the star salespeople.

During a reorganization effort, one company found that 44 employees critical to the company's success were likely to leave.

Risk heat map for European industrial company, figures indicate number of employees in category (total = 492)

		Low risk	Medium risk		High risk	
High	Unique skills/knowledge; a pivotal person in the organization	37	22	9	**8**	**2**
	Important resource whose specific skills/knowledge require careful attention	69	50	39	**15**	**19**
Difficulty in replacing this person	Important resource, but person's competencies are shared and not at risk	74	28	21	14	14
	General competencies in own area	10	22	6	13	13
Low	No specific competencies; easy to find in the market	3	1	2	3	3
		0	25	50	75	100

Probability of person leaving organization, %

Based on market demand for employee's skills, latest salary trends, existing competitive offers, family situation, and known preferences and concerns.

Once HR and line managers have generated a thoughtful and more inclusive list of key players (usually 30 to 45 percent of all employees), they can begin to prioritize groups and individuals for targeted retention measures—in our experience, 5 to 10 percent of the workforce. The key is to view each employee through two lenses: first, the impact his or her departure would have on the business, given the focus of the change effort and his or her role in it; and second, the probability that the employee in question might leave.

When a European industrial company conducted this exercise, it mapped the outputs on a risk matrix. The results were sobering. The company had been launching a new centralized trading unit—requiring almost all traders and their support staff to relocate, with half of them heading to another country—and was steadily losing people. The risk matrix revealed that another 104 people were likely to leave. Among them were 44 employees who were critical for the success of the trading unit. To be sure, some were traders but most were IT, finance, and administrative staff with unique knowledge of the unit's systems.

2. Mind-sets matter

One-size-fits-all retention packages are usually unsuccessful in persuading a diverse group of key employees to stay. Instead, companies should tailor retention approaches to the mind-sets and motivations of specific employees (as well as to the express nature of the changes involved).

When executives at the European industrial company looked beyond their standard retention package (bonuses plus compensation for the costs of the move) and focused instead on the needs of individual employees, they found a more nuanced situation than they had anticipated. Among the key people at risk were two main groups with two different mind-sets.[1] One consisted of individuals who were worried about relocating because it would uproot their families. The people in the other, more career-driven group didn't mind living and working abroad

but wondered, as they faced change in any event, whether staying or searching for another employer would best further their careers.

In one-on-one conversations with the people in the family-oriented group, managers explored specific concerns and discussed how the company could add to the measures already in place to increase the likelihood of retaining these individuals. On the menu of incentives: an increase in base pay, assistance in finding schools and kindergartens for their children, career counseling for their spouses, language training, and alternative work arrangements so employees could work at home or commute instead of relocating.

Meanwhile, in the conversations with the career-driven people, managers offered them a cash bonus but focused primarily on the organiza-

[1] The number of groups will vary according to a company's specific situation. We have observed circumstances where employers have identified up to six distinct employee segments.

tional chart of the new, centralized unit, which had been designed from scratch. For people who had held senior roles in their local organization, it was essential, for example, to learn about their new responsibilities and how many direct reports they would have; for many of the more junior people a key question was who their bosses would be. Also high on the agenda was a dialogue with each individual about his or her future career and leadership opportunities in the context of the unit's new strategy.

This targeted approach, which cost just one-quarter as much as the broad financial incentives plan the company had previously applied, succeeded in stabilizing the new unit. One year after its launch, some 80 percent of the staff who received special attention had started to work in the new location—a significantly higher share than for the group that didn't receive this attention. Since its founding, the unit has increased its sales by more than 30 percent and its earnings before interest and taxes (EBIT) by more than 90 percent.

3. Retention is about more than money

As the European industrial company's experience suggests, financial incentives play an important role in retention—but money alone won't do the trick. Praise from one's manager, attention from leaders, frequent promotions, opportunities to lead projects, and chances to join fast-track management programs are often more effective than cash. Indeed, a 2009 *McKinsey Quarterly* survey found that executives, managers, and employees rate these five nonfinancial incentives among the six most effective motivators when the main objective of the exercise is retaining people.[2]

One financial services firm undertaking a recent cost-cutting initiative elected to use *only* nonfinancial measures—including leadership-development programs—to retain the pivotal players it had identified as being at risk of departure. One year later, none of those players had quit.

Leadership opportunities are a powerful incentive in any sector. In a pharmaceuticals merger aimed at building the North American acquirer's presence in Europe, some 50 middle managers from the acquired company accepted invitations to join trans-Atlantic teams with key roles in integrating the two organizations and developing business strategy. The chance to network with the acquirer's senior people and develop leadership skills during the two-year program signaled to these high-potential employees—in many cases, people who had been slated for promotion before the merger was announced—that they had a promising future in the new organization. For the acquirer's senior executives, one benefit was the opportunity to assess first hand a potential next wave of top management talent. The program was one part of a carefully designed communication and engagement plan

[2]See Martin Dewhurst, Matthew Guthridge, and Elizabeth Mohr, "Motivating people: Getting beyond money," mckinseyquarterly.com, November 2009.

that made it possible to sustain the energy of the 50,000-person strong workforce during the merger. The company ultimately needed to offer only 750 targeted employees a financial incentive.

When financial incentives *are* required, it is important to design them appropriately and use them in a targeted way. For example, one-third of the retention bonus during a merger might be paid to pivotal staff even before the deal is closed, with the remaining two-thirds to be paid out a year later—dependent in part on the recipients meeting defined performance criteria such as the successful transfer of systems from the acquired company.

●   ●   ●

Targeting retention measures at the right people using a tailored mix of financial and nonfinancial incentives is crucial for managing organizational transitions that achieve long-term business success; it's also likely to save money.

Still, executives mustn't view employee retention as a one-off exercise where it's sufficient to get the incentives packages right. Rather, best-practice approaches build on continuous attention and timely communication every step of the way to help employees make sense of the uncertainty inherent in organizational change. Ultimately, what many employees want most of all is clarity about their future with the company. Creating that clarity requires significant hands-on effort from managers, including the ongoing work of tracking progress so that companies can quickly intervene when problems arise. **o**

Sabine Cosack is a consultant in McKinsey's Vienna office; Matt Guthridge is an associate principal in the London office, where Emily Lawson is a principal. Copyright © 2010 McKinsey & Company. All rights reserved.

Extra Point

Tricks for taking charge

Stanford University management professor
Bob Sutton says it's an illusion that
the boss is truly in control, and suggests seven
"tricks" for enhancing that perception:

1
Talk more than others, but not the whole time.
At least in Western countries, people who talk first and most are seen as leaders—the blabbermouth theory. But if you talk the whole time, people will find you a bully, a bore, or both.

2
Interrupt occasionally—
and don't let others interrupt you too much. You can augment your power by winning "interruption wars" at key junctures in meetings.

3
Cross your arms when you talk.
When people make this gesture, they persist longer and generate more solutions while working on difficult tasks. By crossing your arms, you send yourself a message to crank up the grit and confidence—but crossing them too often and intensely can make you look inaccessible and unfriendly.

4
Use positive self-talk.
People who make encouraging statements to themselves enjoy higher self-esteem and performance. The most effective such talk focuses on encouraging yourself ("you've done this before") and applying specific strategies ("lean hard, now").

5
Try a flash of anger occasionally.
The strategic use of outbursts, snarling looks, and hand gestures such as pointing and jabbing generates an aura of competence in small doses with proper precautions. But spewing out constant venom undermines your authority and earns you a well-deserved reputation as a jerk.

6
If you aren't sure whether to sit or to stand, stand.
This point is especially crucial for a new boss. Standing up signals that you are in charge and encourages others to accept your authority. Whether you sit or stand, place yourself at the head of the table.

7
Surrender some power or status, but make sure everyone knows that you did so freely.
One of the most effective ways to show that you are both powerful and benevolent is to take a status symbol for yourself and give it to others. A CEO I work with had a huge corner office, but when he became aware of a space crunch, he moved to a much smaller space so that four employees could share the big one.

For more on taking charge, see Sutton's article, "Why good bosses tune in to their people," on page 86; Ian Davis's "Letter to a newly appointed CEO," on page 70; and a firsthand account of stepping into the top job from Juniper Networks CEO Kevin Johnson on page 78.